GAME OVER: ABC'S OF ETERNAL LIFE JESUS'S ROLE IN HUMAN CREATION

The new Gospel revelations series 3

**The New Gospel Revelations Series *of* the
New Christianity of Christ Essentials Made Easy.**
The Words and Works of Christ Decoded

Festus Enumah M.D.

The New Gospel Revelations Series of the New Christianity of
Christ *Essentials* Made Easy
The Words and Works of Jesus Christ Decoded
Game Over: ABC's of Eternal Life Jesus's Role in Human Creation
The New Gospel Revelations Series 3
Copyright © 2016 Festus Enumah M.D.
United States Library of Congress Catalog Card: TXu 2-005-841 Date 03-11-2016

For information regarding permission, write to:
Festus Enumah, M.D.
1629 10th Avenue. Columbus. GA 31901. USA
The Library of Congress of United States in Cataloging
Festus Enumah M.D.
1629 10th Avenue. Columbus, Georgia, 31901. USA

ISBN: 0692792112
ISBN 13: 9780692792117
Library of Congress Control Number: 2016917059
Festus Enumah, Columbus, Georgia

DEDICATION

This book is dedicated to all who seek knowledge of the words and works of Jesus Christ

TABLE OF CONTENTS

INTRODUCTION

I came that they might have life and have it more
abundantly.

—Jesus. John 10:10

Eternal life stands at the central point, next to the Kingdom of God in all the preaching and demonstrations of Jesus Christ. We have not really grasped the meaning of those words and the illustrations connected with them. The definitions we have given to eternal life as life after death that gives the resurrected spiritual body a new life as to be able to live with Jesus Christ and His Father forever, are inadequate and missed the basic fundamentals of what Christ attempted to reveal to us on eternal life and why we need it now. His metaphoric and figurative words on eternal life are not enough to have a full grasp on the meaning of eternal life and its applicability in our lives in this 21st century. The abundant texts in the Gospel of John revealed that eternal life as preached by Christ positioned it as starting in this earthly life. "Verily, verily, I say unto you, He that heareth my word, and believeth in Him that sent me, hath everlasting life, and shall not come into condemnation; but is passed from death unto life." (John 5:24) However, there were no revelations in those texts that revealed the true meaning of eternal life and why we need it. The mysteries of eternal life remained hidden as no further light was thrown on Jesus's demonstrations on eternal life since immediately after the crucible of Christianity to the present time.

A grounded knowledge of what is eternal life carries with it the reason to live and the reason to die. It allows one to have a glimpse into the divine creative element that originated from the Spirit of the Father that has the ultimate and deepest influence on human life. Jesus Christ branded that divine creative element in the Spirit of His Father and called it Eternal Life! Sometimes He simply refers to it as Life.

> *For as the Father hath life in himself; so hath he given to the Son to have life in himself.*

—John 5:26

> *As thou hast given him power over all flesh, that he should give eternal life to as many as thou hast given him.*

—John 17:2

Jesus has this life in Him and was given the authority to dispense it to human souls. Today, Jesus is still endowing human souls with that creative Spirit that originated from His Father, to whomsoever would like to receive it. He is not waiting for us to die before we can receive it.

Eternal life distanced itself from the Christian's eschatological expectation of the life that starts after the second coming of Jesus Christ and the resurrection of the dead. It does not wait for Christ to come back again and establish His spiritual Kingdom on earth. It dissociated itself from both the salvation of the Jews and the Christian concepts of salvation. It is given to us not because we have sinned and not purchased by the blood of Christ. That gift was given to mankind before Christ came. Many people received it during His mission before His death.

What is eternal life and why we need it will remain unintelligible, elusive and hidden if we do not know the meaning of Jesus's Kingdom of God and develop complete vision of His epic miracle of the earthly stages of human creation. It breached into the mysteries of Jesus's Kingdom of God, revealing the latent divine contents of that Kingdom and its power as it propels the creative element of this life in human souls that inherited it, along the creative trajectory, as the soul strives, not only to be as perfect as the Father, but also to be fully created in the spiritual image of the risen Christ. Eternal life holds the key to Jesus's role in human creation. When what is eternal life is revealed, the entire words of Christ and His practical demonstrations on the meaning of it and why we need it becomes more comprehensible.

Jesus used the apostles, the dead people and Himself as models to reveal the mysteries of eternal life. In this epiphany, I have concentrated my efforts to reveal those mysteries in an easy way so everyone would understand the essentials of eternal life by illuminating Jesus's demonstrations on eternal life and by deep exploration of His words on it. Jesus's encounter with the rich young ruler who came to Him and asked Him, "Good Master, what good things shall I do, that I may have eternal life?" (Mark 10:17-31), provided an excellent introductory platform to the subject. It is the greatest story in the Gospel as it forayed into the mysteries of Jesus Kingdom of God and its connection with eternal life.

We have all seen rich people, have we not? You may be one of them. Your neighbor may be one of them. We have encountered many rich rulers-Presidents, Heads of States, Governors, Mayors, and tribal rulers. We have read many publications on the habits and secrets of the rich. Every year Forbes Magazine publishes the list of four hundred richest people in the world. Today, the ultrahigh-networth individuals have more than $46 trillion in assets. In reality, if you have a bank account that is not in the red, I count you as a rich person for this simple reason: billions of people do not have a bank account and their net worth is less than ten dollars. They live on less than one dollar a day. Those people think of you as a rich person. The story of the rich man who came to Jesus to ask Him how he could obtain eternal life is your story and not just the story of the rich as we perceive it in today's world. On His way to Jerusalem, Jesus was confronted by a rich man who said to Him: "Good Master, what good things shall I do, that I may have eternal life?" (Matthew 19:16) Why did the rich man ask Jesus and not one of the Jewish religious leaders, what he must do that he may have eternal life? The reason is simple: eternal life and the Kingdom of God were the two core messages that Jesus preached everywhere. Jesus portrayed Himself, not just as an authority on eternal life but also that He has the power to give it. (John 3:15; 6:54; 10:28; 17:2) Peter had confessed that the words of Christ are the words of eternal life. The young rich ruler went to the right person to gain knowledge of this eternal life. Jesus claimed He got the authority from His Father to give this eternal life to mankind who are willing to receive it.

Jesus used that opportunity to introduce His Kingdom of God and the demands of morals and the ethics of that Kingdom by telling the rich man to keep the commandments: "Thou shall do no murder. Thou shall not commit adultery. Thou shall not steal. Thou shall not bear false witness. Honor thy father and thy mother. Thou shall love thy neighbor as thyself." (Matthew 19:18, 19) The young man, a true Israelite, who had since childhood obeyed all the commandments, whose morals and ethics were beyond reproach, replied:

"All these things have I kept from my youth up, what lack I yet"

Jesus looked at the young man who kneeled before Him with compassion. He found a man whom He loved as one of His ordained apostles. Jesus must have known what the rich young ruler did for his people. The fear and love of God and his neighbors, integrity, unbiased judgment, support of his community were the hallmarks of his character that prompted his people to elect him as a ruler. As was reported, Jesus loved him. He lifted up His face and turning to the young man said: "You lack one thing: sell all you have, distribute to the poor and you will have treasures in heaven; and come and follow me."(Luke 18:22) That was a big surprise. What Jesus just did by that utterance pulled the rug off from the platform of moral and ethical commandments as a prerequisite for eternal life. There is more to eternal life that superseded moral and ethical professionalism. When the young man heard what Jesus said, he went away grieved: for he had great possessions. It was a perfect test for apostleship for the rich young ruler. Jesus looked at the audience and said to His apostles:

Verily I say unto you, that a rich man shall hardly enter the kingdom of Heaven. It is easier for a camel to go through the eye of a needle; than for a rich man to enter into the kingdom of God.

—Matthew 19:23, 24

What strikes me with interest is not what the apostles asked Jesus: "If a rich man cannot enter into the Kingdom of God, who then can be saved?" The rich young ruler rejected the offer to follow Christ. It was a subtle rejection of the Spirit of Christ. To reject Christ is to reject His Kingdom of God and the Father that sent Him, The mystery of the story will unfold as you read what Jesus had in stock for the young man if he had sold everything and followed Jesus. Simon Peter and the other apostles had left all their earthly possessions and followed Jesus. Peter had asked Jesus: "Behold, we have forsaken all, and followed thee; what shall we have therefore?" (Matthew 19:27) Jesus replied:

Verily I say unto you, There is no man that hath left house, or parents or brethren, or wife or children, for the Kingdom of God's sake,

Who shall not receive manifold more in this present time, and in the world to come life everlasting.

—Luke 18:20, 30

The rewards bestowed on the twelve holy apostles-the twelve blessed jewels of His Kingdom-were not only everlasting life but also the privilege to be with Him in His Father's Kingdom. "I go to prepare a place for you that where I am, there ye may be also." (John 14:2, 3) "Father, I will that they also, whom thou hast given me, be with me where I am; that they may behold my glory, which thou hast given me: for thou lovedst me before the foundation of the world." (John 17:24)

What makes this story great is that it actually formed a framework that revealed the core divine element-eternal life-in Jesus's Kingdom of God and how to obtain it by following Jesus. It would seem at this stage that Peter ventured on this chimerical undertaking of following Jesus in the hope of earthly reward. However it was subsequently reported that as Jesus taught in Capernaum, many of His disciples left. Jesus turned to the apostles and said: "Will you also go away?" It was Simon Peter who replied; Lord, to whom shall we go? Thou hast the words of eternal life." (John 6:68) Peter was at that time not just thinking of his earthly reward. He was also thinking of the gift of eternal life. The apostles could have made our task easy by asking Jesus, "what is the Kingdom of God and why must the rich man follow you to have eternal life?"

The rich man could have sold his possessions and distributed them to the poor. But he chose not to do so. He clung to his earthly possessions. What kind of man did he become after the encounter with Jesus? Did he move on as usual with his behavior firmly rooted in the grass-roots in the traditional laws and custom of his people? Perhaps he became humbled like the rich man Zacchaeus who invited Jesus to his house and confesses to Him:

"Behold, Lord, the half of my goods I give to the poor; and if I have taken anything from any man by false accusation, I restore him fourfold." (Luke 19:8) A certain centurion, a man of authority, affluence and power, whose servant was healed by Jesus, built a synagogue in Capernaum for the people. (Luke 7: 2-10) It is within the realm of possibility that the rich young ruler had a change of heart and built a synagogue for his community and sold half or all of his possessions and gave the proceeds to the poor. We will never know. However, we do know that in A.D. 66-70, about forty years after the rich man met with Jesus, and in A.D. 132-135, the Roman army besieged and destroyed the province of Judea and the city of Jerusalem. The inhabitants were either killed or carried into captivity as slaves. The rich man-dead or alive during the first war against the Romans- lost all his possessions as they were destroyed by the Roman army. When the Roman army invaded Jerusalem, the apostles who left all and followed Jesus were outside Jerusalem preaching the Gospel of the Kingdom of God as they perceived it at that time and spreading the news that God resurrected Jesus Christ.

What shall it profit a man if he gains the whole world and lose his soul

—Jesus. Mark 8:36.

The interpretation of the above statement from Jesus is simple-What is the value of abundant earthly possessions to a man who must die and leave all behind?

The epistemology of eternal life and the Kingdom of God that surfaced in this great story makes it plain that morals and ethics of the good, even selling all your earthly possessions and distributing them to the poor, are just a prologue to the inheritance of what Jesus and His Father had planned: the endowment of eternal life to human souls. They had been doing that since the first human was created. The plan was to reveal what they have been doing. Knowledge is an effective tool that will open the door of inspiration for many people to receive that life. Jesus turned the story of the young man into His own story by projecting Himself as the platform the young man must use for eternal life. He must follow Him and learn from him all aspects of eternal life. Jesus had turned the request of the young man to the revelation of the connection of His kingdom of God with eternal life. The invitation to sell your possessions and follow Him was not a mouse trap Jesus used to induce or intimidate people who seek eternal life. "Children, how hard is it for them that trust in riches to enter into the Kingdom of God." (Mark 19:24) However, Jesus quickly added that: "With men it is impossible, but not with God; for with God all things are possible." (Mark 10:27) By seeking to follow Jesus, what was held in secret on what God is creating and how He is creating mankind through Jesus is revealed. The story of the young man became the story of the Kingdom of God and the epitome of the earthly stages of human creation that Jesus refused to reveal that opens the portal of eternal life. The call to the young man to follow Him was an invitation to invest in eternal life by following the Father's appointed Chief Executive Officer of eternal life. It was an invitation to the young rich ruler to follow Him and have a taste of His Kingdom. It was an invitation to follow Him and witness the greatest of all His miracles: the everlasting miracle of the earthly stages of human creation.

A complete book could be written on that story of the young ruler with Jesus. It forays into all aspects of the Gospel-who His Father is, who Jesus is, why He came, what He did, and why He is indispensible in our acquisition of the Kingdom of God and eternal life. What started as a prologue for what I recovered in the Gospel, illuminated the words and deeds of Jesus that were not only applicable to the activities of the people of His time but also to all human activities of the present generation-the poor, the rich and the rulers of the people. It is sad to point out though, that today, the most important priority of most of the poor, the rich and the rulers of the people, is not eternal life, but financial security. Deep exploration of the encounter of the young ruler with Jesus will surely catapult one into the spiritual world of Jesus and make the quest for financial security irrelevant. The story was an introduction to:

> The intrinsic value of eternal life in human life
> The connection of the Kingdom of God with eternal life
> The revelations of an essential creative element in the Kingdom of God
> Why we need eternal life and how to get it

Despite all obstacles, Jesus precisely executed the will of His Father. They were epic proclamations and demonstrations that revealed more mysteries of His Kingdom of God. When completely dissected out and deeply explored, using the Gospel as the source of this vital knowledge, Jesus's words and His demonstrations on what is eternal life, why we need it, how do we know we have it, its connection with His Kingdom of God and His role in human creation unfolded and revealed deeper mysteries of that Kingdom:

> His Father as the source of the eternal life
> Jesus Christ as the authority to give eternal life to human souls
> Eternal life as a divine creative component in Jesus's kingdom of God
> Earthly phase of eternal life in human souls who entered into His Kingdom
> After death phase of the eternal life for those who possessed it before they died
> The role of the Father in human creation

The role of Jesus in human creation
God, the Father of Christ, as the only true living God.

There will be many obstacles-wealth and earthly possessions-as was clearly portrayed in this story-and in Jesus's temptations by Satan. Do not be afraid to follow He who "has the words of eternal life" and came to the world that we may have life and have it abundantly. In this journey, let the true Gospel texts be your guide book. It is my hope that this book will be a supplement to the Gospel in revealing the real missing dimensions in knowledge of Jesus's Kingdom of God, how it is linked with eternal life and Jesus's role in human creation. Welcome on board. Fasten your seat belt. It is the journey of your soul. Allow it to be touched by the Spirit of Christ, and be the recipient of that one promise of the Father for all mankind. Good luck and safe trip. The Chief Captain is Jesus Christ. Let the journey begin!

Follow Me. Learn of Me.

—Jesus

You can help
There is a voice of our human spirit within us of that great promise and that out there in the spiritual realm, is the home of mankind. But that realm is unsearchable. We cannot Google it. If you find the answers to what is eternal life and how mankind can harness it's promises, then publicize it, put it up on Billboards, twitter it to everyone with I-phones, advertise it on television when the public is glued to the screen watching NFL or world soccer games; send out agents to all parts of the world to give the people of all nations the Good News. This is precisely what I intend to do in my lifetime on the ground that I found the answers in the Gospel of Jesus Christ. You can help in the dissemination of the

vital information. Jesus-in words and deeds-gave the answer to all those perplexing questions on eternal life and concentrated His efforts on how mankind can get it. Jesus was sent down as a human being. It enabled Him to give us a practical demonstration of the earthly phase of eternal life by His earthly life style. Jesus allowed Himself to be put to death in disgrace, in accordance with the will and the commandment of His Father that we may know the intrinsic value of human life and also see the prototype of the image of that life after death. In doing so, Jesus revealed Himself and His Father who sent Him. Jesus sent out His apostles to spread the Good News of this life and to publicize the vital knowledge of Him and His Father to all nations of the world. Today, with the availability of our current information technology, we can be better messengers and publishers than the apostles.

CHAPTER 1

MYSTERIES OF ETERNAL LIFE

And this is life eternal, that they might know thee the only true God, and Jesus Christ, whom thou hast sent.

—John 17:3

For as the Father hath life in himself; so hath he given to the Son to have life in himself.

—John 5:26

I am the way, the truth and the life.

—Jesus

The story of the man with advanced pancreatic cancer. The year was in 1980. As I walked into the patient's room to break the news that he had incurable pancreatic cancer, I felt like a man with an impossible mission. After discussing all the radiologic reports and my clinical findings, I broke the news to the patient and his wife that he had an advanced cancer of the pancreas.

His wife broke down crying and the patient remained silent. With tears still rolling down her eyes, she asked:

"Where is God? I have prayed every day for my husband to live. He is a good man."

Then the patient broke his silence and asked:

"Doctor, is there anything you can do to remove the cancer?"

"There is nothing anyone can do to remove it at this stage of the disease." I replied

The patient knew that he was doing to die and asked:

"How long will I live?"

There are many similar stories like my patient's story. We see them every day. We are witnesses to the evil activities in this world that destroy human lives. We end up asking the same question that generations before us asked: what is the meaning of earthly human life? Has this human life any intrinsic value? If it has an intrinsic value, we can use that information to give authentic hope to people like my patient and others who are about to die. What then is eternal life, why do we need it and how do we get it? What are the proofs for it? These are the most important but perplexing topics in human history. Human life is still a great mystery. Human origin and its destiny is still an inscrutable mystery. With what was handed down to us on eternal life by Christianity of today, we cannot pierce into the real mysteries of human life or the real meaning of eternal life as preached by Christ.

But we speak the wisdom of God in a mystery, even the hidden wisdom, which God ordained before the world unto our glory: Which

none of the princes of this world knew: for had they known it, they would not have crucified the Lord of glory. But as it is written, Eye hath not seen, nor ear heard, neither have entered into the heart of man, the things which God hath prepared for them that love him.

—1 Corinthians 2:7-9

What then is this hidden glory for mankind? The Gospel of Jesus is not about the end of the world but about the mysteries of human creation and the role of His Father and Himself in that process. The promise of eternal life by Jesus is everywhere in that Gospel. The Gospel knows of only one objective: to get all people on this planet Earth enter into Jesus's Kingdom of God, activate it, inherit eternal life, have experience of it and manifest their personal experiences of that Kingdom. Eternal life is one of the mysteries of Jesus's Kingdom of God. Jesus expounded the meaning of His Kingdom of God and eternal life by using Himself as a model in His epic miracle of the earthly stages of human creation. The Gospel knows of only one goal: eternal life, both the earthly life and the after death life for all mankind. The Gospel seeks to reveal only one vital knowledge: the knowledge of the Father and Jesus Christ whom He sent to this world and who we are, why we are here and where we are going. The words and works of Jesus Christ in the Gospel are all about human creation and protection of what His Father and Himself are creating. These goals and the objective hold the key to all the mysteries and the revelations of the words and works of Jesus Christ and why His Father sent Him to this world. The Gospel in brief is the revelation of the knowledge of Jesus's Kingdom of God, the proof of the certainty of earthly and after death eternal life, the recognition of the Father as the living true God and the acknowledgment of Jesus Christ as the voice of the Father with authority to endow human souls with eternal life and participate in creating human beings.

I came that they might have life and have it more abundantly.

—Jesus. John 10:10

What is eternal life and why do we need it?

The Kingdom of God and eternal life dominated Jesus's teaching. Jesus shadowed the meaning of His Kingdom of God and its mysteries in the eternal life, in parables, metaphors and symbolic utterances related to that life. Jesus encouraged the people to seek the Kingdom of God and its righteousness without verbally connecting it with creation. Subsequently, in the attempt to disclose the meaning of His Kingdom of God, Jesus engaged Himself in demonstrating it in His earthly lifestyle and in the performance of the miracle of the earthly stages of human creation. He used Himself as the model. We all missed the vital information the miracle provided. His parables and teaching on eternal life was even harder to comprehend. Jesus claimed to be the living bread from heaven and the water of life. As Jesus expounded to the Jews on how to get eternal life by eating the bread from heaven and His flesh and drinking His blood, many of them, including many of His disciples deserted Him because they could not understand what He was saying. (John 6:51-66) Jesus accused the Jews that they rejected His invitation to come to Him and have eternal life. (John 5:40) What was missing in all the sayings of Jesus on eternal life is this: why do we need it now and what do we do with it? Again, in all His public proclamations on eternal life, Jesus did not verbally connect it with the earthly stages of human creation. He gave a public display of why we need it by His epic miracle of the earthly stages of human creation. Who could understand it at that time?

Eternal life is more than living forever after we have died. You may live forever in the Kingdom of the dead or in hell. Living forever with Gods, whose promises are often broken and unfulfilled is no life at all. Living forever with the Gods of the Greco-Roman

Empire, or with the forgotten Gods of great Empires, is no life at all. Living forever with the Devil-although no one has seen the Devil-is no life at all. Living forever in Hell is not a life. Jesus redefined immortality of the human souls with spiritual life of His Father during our earthly and after earthly life and channeled it to the new God, His Father and Himself. The journey of the human soul is the journey of the soul with this life with Christ to His Father.

We can have a glimpse into the mysteries of eternal life and have knowledge why we need it now by expounding Jesus's definition of external life.

> *And this is life eternal, that they might know thee the only true God, and Jesus Christ, whom thou hast sent.*

> —Jesus. John 17:3

Jesus's definition of eternal life when viewed with the lens of His Kingdom of God and His epic miracle of human creation, points to the knowledge of His Father and Himself as Creators: that you may know the Father, the only true God and Jesus Christ as the Creators. Eternal life is the creative divine element in the Spirit of the Father, given to us as a gift through Christ. Eternal life is within us. We need it to be participants in our earthly stages of human creation, as proclaimed, prescribed and demonstrated by Christ in His miracle of life. In the transcendental transformation of the human soul in its creative evolution as it seeks to be fully created to achieve that goal. As the human soul with the eternal life positions itself in the human creative trajectory, it is powered by Jesus's Kingdom of God. The house within you was already near completion by the time you die. What is eternal life is revealed when you have knowledge of the creative element embedded in His Spirit that was given to Christ who endowed us with that Spirit.

That knowledge of the creative power of the Spirit of His Father that is in Him was revealed by Jesus's everlasting miracle of human creation. He used Himself as the model. Eternal life, the creative divine element from His Father, given to all mankind through Christ, positioned itself on the trajectory of all the earthly stages of human creative process and continues to be the dominant spiritual life after resurrection for those who inherited it before death. This is the mystery of eternal life. Jesus had this eternal life in His human soul as a human being, proclaimed it, lived it by His earthly life examples, and demonstrated it in His epic miracle of the earthly stages of human creation.

> *For as the Father hath life in himself; so hath he given to the Son to have life in himself.*

> —John 5:26

This creative life in the Spirit of the Father in Christ is eternal life. Jesus came to give us the same life in Him and in the Father. We are not yet fully created. Earthly life is a phase in human creation. If we are fully created, the gift from His Father to human souls will be worthless. If we have to receive it after death, then, it would be of no value for the Father to send Jesus to give us a practical demonstration of what they have been doing with human souls during our earthly life. They could have waited till after we have died to give us that life. In the last chapter of this epiphany, I discussed what would happen to people who died without this vital information of eternal life.

> *I am the way, the truth, and the life: no man cometh unto the Father, but by me.*

> —John 14:6

Eternal life is within us now. We do not have to die before we get it. Jesus gave a practical demonstration what this eternal life is, and how to obtain it by the epitome of His life, spiritualization of human souls with His Spirit and by His death and resurrection. You have to pass through the yoke of Jesus's kingdom of God as to inherit the earthly form of eternal life and advance through death and resurrection, as demonstrated by Jesus Himself as to fulfill the requirements for after death eternal life. Jesus claimed that to enter into the earthly phase of human creative trajectory that leads to eternal life without His Spirit of Christ is as impossible as it is to push a camel through the eye of the needle. (Matthew 19:19:24; Mark 10:25; Luke 8:25) We can achieve nothing by ourselves-no eternal life, no fellowship with His Father- without the Spirit of Christ.

> *Take my yoke upon you, and learn of me; for I am meek and lowly in heart: and ye shall find rest unto your souls. For my yoke is easy, and my burden is light.*

> —Matthew 11:29-30

To take His yoke is to be bequeathed with the Spirit of the Father through Him. Jesus gave the assurance that His Spirit is easy to get and that it will give peace and tranquility to our souls as we embark on the journey to eternal life. Eternal life is the paradise of the human souls striving to express itself as fully created spiritual creature with the Spirits of the Father through Jesus Christ. It initiates, sustains and guides the human soul in its timeless transformation to both the spiritual image of the risen Christ and all spiritual experiences associated with it.

> *And we know that the Son of God is come, and hath given us an understanding, that we may know him that is true, and we are in*

him that is true, even in his Son Jesus Christ. This is the true God, and eternal life.

—1 John 5:20

And this is the record that God hath given to us eternal life, and this life is in his Son. He that hath the Son hath life; and he that hath not the Son of God hath not life. These things have I written unto you that believe on the name of the Son of God; that ye may know that ye have eternal life, and that ye may believe on the name of the Son of God.

—1 John 5:11-13

The creative evolutionary process of human life that I have been presenting in this treatise planned by the Father and executed and demonstrated by Christ in His miracle of human life, catapulted the evolved fully created mankind-a prototype of the risen Christ-to an infinite union with the Father and Jesus Christ. In reminiscence, the trajectory of eternal life leads to one direction only: divine trinity of the human souls with the Spirit of the Father and Jesus Christ. This is the ultimate glory of the human soul. The rewards of eternal life are portrayed in the Beatitudes.

Blessed are the poor in spirit: for theirs is the kingdom of heaven.
   Blessed are they that mourn: for they shall be comforted.
   Blessed are the meek: for they shall inherit the earth.
   Blessed are they which do hunger and thirst after righteousness: for they shall be filled.
   Blessed are the merciful: for they shall obtain mercy.
   Blessed are the pure in heart: for they shall see God.
   Blessed are the peacemakers: for they shall be called the children of God.

Blessed are they which are persecuted for righteousness' sake: for theirs is the kingdom of Heaven.

—Matthew 5:3-10

I have intentionally highlighted the third Beatitude to point out the fact that the promise of the Father that Jesus revealed has nothing to do with inheriting land on this planet Earth. However, the God of Israel promised a permanent land-the Promised Land in Palestine-to the Jews. The Father that Jesus revealed is not the Jewish God. The only things the meek have inherited on this planet Earth are the slums, the unfertile lands, and the refugee camps. Here again, the introduction of that third Beatitude is to force us to read the Beatitudes with the Jewish lens. Part of the Beatitudes fell among the weeds. Shall we remove the weeds? Jesus said no! You may damage the roots of the other seven as was revealed in the parable of the Tares. (Matthew 13:28) Now that I have pointed it out, I will continue on the epiphany of eternal life.

Jesus knew what would be the final reward for the apostles and all who had forsaken everything and had followed Him: "that they all may be one; as thou, Father art in me, and I in thee, that they also may be one in us, that the world may believe that thou hast sent me." (John 17:21) That was part of Jesus's prayer to His Father for us and the apostles. However, revealed in that prayer is what awaits all humanity. The divine Trinity of the human soul was echoed by one of His apostles: "That which we have seen and heard, declare us unto you, that ye also may have fellowship with us; and truly our fellowship is with the Father, and with His Son Jesus Christ." (1 John 1:3) The twelve holy apostles already got this reward. The blending of the spirits of the twelve apostles and our spirits in the new divine Trinity was clearly outlined by Jesus: "My prayer is not for them alone. I pray also for them who will believe in me through their message; that all of them may be one, Father, just as you are

9

in me and I am in you, may they also be in us. Neither pray I for these alone, but for them also which shall believe in me through their word; That they all may be one; as thou, Father, art in me, and I in thee, that they also may be one in us: that the world may believe that thou hast sent me. And the glory which thou gavest me I have given them; that they may be one, even as we are one: I in them, and thou in me, that they may be made perfect in one; and that the world may know that thou hast sent me, and hast loved them, as thou hast loved me. " (John 17:20-23)

This is the story of the terrestrial and extraterrestrial journey of the human spirit. Both the human life on earth and in heaven is bound together with the Spirit of Christ and His Father and cannot be broken. Jesus asked, "What shall it profit a man if he gains the whole world and loses his soul?" The interpretation is self-explanatory: of what use are all the earthly wealth and power to a person if he or she fails to inherit the eternal and everlasting glory of the divine Trinity of the soul with Him and the Father?

The Spirit of God, the Father, given to all humans through Christ, is the potent precursor element on the earthly phase of the evolutionary trajectory of human creation. The human soul, empowered by this gift, as it prepares itself for eternal life, looked at the cross and did not see the 'suffering servant' that was revealed in the Prophetic vision of Isaiah (Isaiah 53) or somebody on the cross, condemned by the Jews, ready to die for our sins in accordance with the Scriptures. (1 Corinthians 15: 3-5) It saw the glory of the cross and what was revealed on the third day, when Christ resurrected Himself as evidence that he can participate in that glory and be a participant in his own creation. It rejoiced, knowing full well that death is not a consequence of human sins or an act of redemption or ransom but a grand station along the human evolutionary creative trajectory that it must pass as to harvest and express its final glory: the eternal life that started in his earthly life and will continue after death.

CHAPTER 2

JESUS'S WORDS ON ETERNAL LIFE

Lord, to whom shall we go? Thou hast the words of Eternal life.

—Peter. John 6:68

The word that I speak to you, they are spirit and they are life.

—John 6:63

If a man loves me, he will keep my words; and my Father will love him, and we will come unto him, and make our abode with him. He that loveth me not keepeth not my sayings: and the word which ye hear is not mine, but the Father's which sent me.

—Jesus, John 14:23-24

I am the good shepherd, and know my sheep, and am known of mine. As the Father knoweth me, even so know I

*the Father: and I lay down my life for the sheep. And other
sheep I have, which are not of this fold: them also I must
bring, and they shall hear my voice; and there shall be one
fold, and one shepherd.*

—John 10:14-16

*My sheep hear my voice, and I know them, and they follow
me: And I give unto them eternal life; and they shall never
perish, neither shall any man pluck them out of my hand.
My Father, which gave them me, is greater than all; and
no man is able to pluck them out of my Father's hand. I
and my Father are one.*

—John 10:27-30

Jesus's words are words of power He used revealing the power of His kingdom of God. Nearly all His miracles were accomplished by verbal commands. Jesus's words focused primarily on revelation of His Father and the works the Father sent Him to do. The words of His commandments exemplified by His earthly life style set the ground for the knowledge of who we are, why we are here and where we are going. Jesus used His words as instruments or the praxis to illuminate and supplement His works on the evolutionary creative trajectory of the human soul in its journey for full spiritual life. Jesus had portrayed Himself as the instrument for this authentic life, planned by His Father for humanity: "I am the way, and the truth, and the life; no one cometh unto the Father but by me." (John 14:6) The words of Jesus are the divine instructions we must use to be participants in the process that brings eternal life. The mystery of the words of Jesus as the instrument for eternal life is revealed if, first, we can understand the meaning of Jesus's Kingdom of God. Second, if we can comprehend Jesus's spiritual words of eternal life verbalized in parables, proverbs, and symbolic expressions and exemplified in His earthly lifestyle. Third, if we can comprehend Jesus's epic miracle of the earthly stages of human creation. Fourth, a deeper understanding of the Father's will for Christ and His purpose for mankind, all set the definitive platforms for full comprehension of Jesus's word on eternal life as proclaimed, prescribed and demonstrated by Him. Jesus had revealed that His words originated from His Father. "The words that I speak unto you, I speak not of myself but the Father that dwelleth in me, He doeth the works." (John 14:10)

Verily, verily, I say unto you, He that heareth my word, and believeth on him that sent me, hath everlasting life, and shall not come into condemnation; but is passed from death unto life.

—John 5:24

Verily, verily, I say unto you, if a man keeps my saying, he shall never see death.

—John 8:51

Jesus's words are spiritual words of life. They are the divine instructions we must use to be participants in the process that brings eternal life. There is a glorious destiny for all mankind. Jesus's epic miracle of the earthly stages of human creation revealed the beginning of that glorious destiny. Jesus's Kingdom of God was involved in it. That Kingdom of God would continue even as of today, to manifest its iridescent divine rays of light in human souls that has experienced it. The light is not from the moon or the sun. It is the light of eternal life-from the Father given to mankind through Christ-that will shine in human hearts. It would continue to light the pathway of our creative journey to the Father, our God.

I *am the Light to the world.*

—Jesus. John 8:12

Believe in the Light that ye may be called the children of the Light.

—Jesus. John 12:36

CHAPTER 3

ETERNAL LIFE AND JESUS'S KINGDOM OF GOD

Eternal life is intimately connected with Jesus's Kingdom of God and human creation. Two thousand years ago, Jesus launched His Kingdom of God. Eternal life also dominated His teaching. Since then the objectives and goals of His kingdom have not changed. The flagship of that kingdom that came was the Spirit of the Father in Jesus Christ. It carries with it the life that was in His Father. "For as the Father hath life in Himself, so hath He given to the Son to have life in himself." (John 5:26) Jesus was given the authority to give this life of the Father in Him to human souls. The life in the Father that was given to Christ carries with it human creative powers. When the human soul is endowed with it, the creative powers are activated if the recipient is willing to receive it. It propels that soul to a creative trajectory for its full spiritual expression. This life in the Father, in Jesus Christ and given to us through Christ as a gift is the Eternal life. It is the potent element in human creation. It is the creative divine element in Jesus's Kingdom of God. To seek and inherit Eternal life, you must first enter into Jesus's Kingdom of God. All other roads are closed. Eternal life is the reward of those who entered into Jesus's Kingdom of God, experienced it, manifested it and are participating in all the earthly stages of human creation with the infinite power of the Kingdom of God as demonstrated by Jesus in the epic miracle of life. Today, how to inherit eternal life has not changed. It is the same as how to be a participant in the Easter experience. It is the same as was demonstrated by the German Chancellor Angela Merkel and her people in dealing with the refugees.

Seek ye after the Kingdom of God and its righteousness and all these (eternal life and all its blessings) *will be added unto you*

The Kingdom of God and eternal life dominated Jesus's words and all His works. Both are linked to human creation. His epic miracle of the earthly stages of human creation was a public demonstration of the infinite power of His Kingdom and the creative nature of eternal life in Him that originated from His Father. Jesus used Himself as the model. In essence, the most important feature of Eternal life, both in its earthly phase and after life is the power of Jesus's Kingdom of God that initiates and sustains the human soul that inherited Eternal life in its creative evolutional development. Human being is a spirit. Jesus's Kingdom of God in human souls, when activated, is the paradise of Eternal life in that soul, striving to express itself as the new spiritual life both here in this world and after death.

I came to give you life and give it to you abundantly.

—Jesus

The mysteries of Jesus's Kingdom of God and eternal life are the mysteries of human creation. Jesus's Kingdom of God, when projected on the evolutionary creative trajectory of human soul, reveals the honor and the glory that awaits the human soul that are active participants of that Kingdom. Eternal life is the reward to those who entered into Jesus's Kingdom of God, experienced it and manifested it. It is the most important earthly creative human experience mankind can develop. The soul of the human spirit before and after death depends on it for survival. It enables the soul to participate in all the earthly stages of human creation as was demonstrated by Christ in His epic miracle of life. The imprint of the Eternal life dominates and illuminates the spiritual human life during the earthly life and after resurrection for those who were willing to receive it. It is the creative divine element that connects all mankind in this world and in the spiritual world after death.

Jesus introduced an innovative divine element-eternal life-on the trajectory of human creation and encrypted it in the mysteries of His Kingdom of God, in His words on Eternal life and in His everlasting miracle of the earthly stages of human creation and walked away. Because of His silence and His secrecy on His Kingdom of God and why we need eternal life in our earthly lives, the interpretations became impassable frontiers in any attempt to gain full knowledge of His words and works on eternal life. But, then again, Jesus may not agree with this reasoning on the ground that He left many imprints in His Gospel that revealed the connection between human nature and its divine life with His Spirit as it strives to be fully created. That He exemplified it by His life style and demonstrated it in His epic miracle of the earthly stages of human creation. His is right. My dear readers, to comprehend the meaning of eternal life, you have to look at it with the lens of Jesus's Kingdom of God and His epic miracle of life.

For the last two thousand years, we were unable to comprehend the protean manifestations of the creative elements in Jesus's Kingdom of God and in the Eternal life and relegated such experiences to afterlife when Jesus will come back, establish His spiritual Kingdom on earth and give us eternal life. We did not see ourselves in any of those spiritual events in our current earthly lives. What was delivered to us was to hope for eternal life after death.

That being justified by His grace, we should be made heirs according to the hope of eternal life.

—Letter of Paul to Titus 3:7

With the information that I have presented here, the words and works of Christ on Eternal life, moved from the platform of imaginations and apocalyptic Hope of Jesus's Kingdom of God that will manifest at the end of the world that brings with it eternal life to all mankind, to the living sparkles of eternal life within the human souls in this life.

The Kingdom of God cometh not without observation; neither shall they say, lo here or lo there! For, behold, the kingdom of God is within you.

—Luke 17:20-21

Jesus went about the villages and cities in Palestine preaching eternal life and gave practical demonstrations on how to get it. He started with the proclamation of His kingdom of God that came and not of salvation. The eternal life that I have been presenting in this treatise is what you see at the end journey of the human soul. When viewed over the timeless period of that journey as it passes through its evolutionary creative processes-the spiritualization of the soul by the Spirit of Christ, death and resurrection-it reveals something that was visible to humans on Easter-a proof-that gave human life an intrinsic value. In this human soul's evolutionary creative journey, as it advances to its full expression as demonstrated by the resurrection of Christ, revealed, what human life is, who we are, why we are here and where we are going. From what was profiled on Easter, it became obvious that human life was not created the way it was reported by Moses in the book of Genesis.

Jesus's everlasting staged miracle of human creation revealed the *modus operandi* of the earthly phase of human creation. When the creative element in Jesus's kingdom of God and His epic miracle of life is comprehended, the exploration to find the Gods who are creating human beings will end. That Game will be over.

To comprehend the mysteries of Jesus's Kingdom of God within human soul is to understand the meaning of Eternal life that is bound with His role in human creation. To activate it is to unlock the mysteries of that life, here on earth and after death that has infinite bound with the Spirits of the Father and Jesus Christ. This is life eternal.

CHAPTER 4

ABC'S OF ETERNAL LIFE

W hen Eternal life is comprehended as I have simplified and decoded the earthly phase of that life, the knowledge of the Father as the source of that life and Jesus Christ as the dispenser of the life to human souls, is revealed. "And this is life eternal, that they might know thee the only true God, and Jesus Christ, whom thou hast sent." (Jesus. John 17:3) With the words and works of Christ the search for eternal life in Paradise ended. That Game is over. The search for it in this 21st century here on Earth just started. The eternal life in human souls is the imprint of divine elements in the Spirits of the Father and Jesus Christ. It carries with it, creative elements and other divine elements that are found in Jesus's Kingdom of God. As the human soul with eternal life cruise along its creative trajectory, it manifests itself, striving to emulate what is in the nature of Jesus and His Father and what they do for all mankind: love that extends to the enemy, forgiveness, mercy, compassion to people who are strangers to us, justice, avoidance of hatred and jealousy and sharing all things with mankind. This divine nature of the Father is in all human souls who have entered into Jesus's Kingdom of God and inherited the eternal life. It enables us not only to have spiritual life but also to be partakers in the nature of the Father.

But I say unto you which hear, Love your enemies, and do good to them which hate you, bless them that curse you, and pray for them which despitefully use you.

—Luke 6:27-28

That command is precisely what Himself and His Father does and will continue to do for all mankind. The human spiritual life, as demonstrated Jesus's earthly life, translates not just a life bound with death, but a life that expresses itself before death. The earthly phase of eternal life continues uninterrupted through death to spiritual life with the Father and Jesus Christ. Death is a transcendental transformation platform along its trajectory. Death has no sting on it and cannot destroy it. The Spirit of the Father is in eternal life. It is a component in Jesus's Kingdom of God. Those who have it in this life, like the seventy men Jesus sent out to preach, must also rejoice because their names are written in heaven. Those who have entered into Jesus's Kingdom of God are those who have the creative elements of the Spirit of the Father that gives spiritual life.

ABC's of Eternal life presented here are pathways to eternal life as proclaimed, prescribed and demonstrated by Christ. They revealed how to be a participant in the creative process that leads to eternal life. Encourage others to do so.

A-Activate Jesus's Kingdom of God within your soul after you have entered into it.

To enter into His Kingdom of God, is to receive the Spirit of the Father in Him. That Spirit of the Father in Him has human creative element in it. The power of Jesus's Kingdom of God, initiates, sustains and propels the human spirit in its creative trajectory as it strives to express the life that is the Father and in Jesus Christ. The authority to dispense to human souls that Spirit of His Father ingrained with creative element of eternal life was given to Him by His Father. "As thou hast given Him power over all flesh, that He should give eternal life to as many as thou hast given Him." (John 17:2) Jesus metaphorically portrayed the *modus operandi* of receiving that gift of His Father through Him as:

Eating His flesh and drinking His blood.

—John 6:54

Eating His bread of life.

—John 6: 33-35, 51

Eating His meat.

—John 6:27

Drinking His water of everlasting life.

—John 4:14; John 7: 37-38

And this is the record that God hath given to us eternal life, and this life is in His Son.

—1 John 5:11

And I give unto them eternal life; and they shall never perish; neither shall any man pluck them out of my hand.

—John 10:28

B-Believe in His Father as the true God and in Jesus Christ.

The belief in Jesus Christ played a very significant role in His ability to perform many miracles. The philology of the belief in

Jesus Christ forayed beyond His power to heal, into an untouched spiritual ground of bequeathing the created human souls with the life of the Father that is in Him as revealed by many of His utterances:

> *"If any man thirst, let him come unto me and drink. He that believeth, as the Scripture hath said, out of his belly shall flow rivers of living water."*
>
> —John 7:37-38

> *"I am the resurrection and the life; he that believeth in me, though he were dead, yet shall he lives. And whosoever liveth and believeth in me shall never die."*
>
> —John 11:25-26

> *"And this is the will of Him that sent me, that every one which seeth the Son, and believeth on him, may have everlasting life; and I will raise him up at the last day."*
>
> —John 6:39

> *"I am the bread of life; he that cometh to me shall never hunger; and he that believeth on me shall never thirst."*
>
> —John 6:35

> *Verily, verily, I say unto you, He that heareth my word, and believeth on him that sent me, hath everlasting life, and shall not come into condemnation; but is passed from death unto life.*
>
> —John 5:24

And this is the will of him that sent me, that every one which seeth the Son, and believeth on him, may have everlasting life: and I will raise him up at the last day.

—John 6:40

Verily, verily, I say unto you, He that believeth on me hath everlasting life.

—John 6:47

Jesus connected eternal life with knowledge of His Father and Himself. (John 17:3). You must have knowledge of whom they are as to truly believe in them. If you have this knowledge as the ground for your belief, then you will be like He is like "a man who built a house, and digged deep, and laid the foundation on a rock: and when the flood arose, the stream beat vehemently upon that house, and could not shake it: for it was founded upon a rock." If you do not have that knowledge as the foundation of your belief, then you are like "a man that without a foundation built a house upon the earth; against which the stream did beat vehemently, and immediately it fell; and the ruin of that house was great." (Luke 6:48-49)

For the apostles and all who believed in him, Jesus prayed to His Father, "That they all may be one; as thou, Father, art in me, and I in thee, that they also may be one in us; that the world may believe that thou hast sent me." (John 17:21) Jesus has the same plan for everyone who entered into His Kingdom, inherited eternal life, experienced it and manifested the features of the nature of the Father that is linked to that life. To enter into His kingdom is to believe in Him and His Father. To believe in Jesus and His Father is to inherit that eternal life that originated from the Father.

C-Canonize the Commandments of the Father, our God and Jesus Christ.

These commandments dominated Jesus's teachings and centered on His Kingdom of God and eternal life. He set the example by obeying those commandments. "If you keep my commandments, you shall abide in my love; even as I have kept my Father's commandments and abide in His love." (John 15:10) The confession of Jesus Christ as the Lord will not bring eternal life without obeying His commandments. Jesus said, "Why call me Lord. Lord and do not what I say."

And thou shall love the Lord thy God with all thy heart, and with all thy soul, and with all thy mind, and with all thy strength: this is the first commandment. And the second is like, namely this, Thou shall love thy neighbor as thyself.

—Mark 12:30-31

A new commandment I give unto you, That ye love one another; as I have loved you, that ye also love one another.

—John 13:34

He that hath my commandments, and keepeth them, he it is that loveth me: and he that loveth me shall be loved of my Father, and I will love him, and will manifest myself to him.

—John 14:21

But I say unto you which hear, Love your enemies, do good to them which hate you, bless them that curse you, and pray for them which despitefully use you.

—Luke 6:27-28

Forgive those that trespass against you.

—(Part of the Lord's Prayer)

Give to him that asketh thee, and from him that would borrow of thee turn not thou away.

—Matthew 5:42

If ye love me, keep my commandments.

—John 14:15

Ye are my friends, if ye do whatsoever I command you.

—John 15:14

If thou wilt enter into life, keep the commandments.

—Matthew 19:17

But seek ye first the kingdom of God, and his righteousness; and all these things shall be added unto you.

—Matthew 6:33

Whosoever therefore shall break one of these least commandments, and shall teach men so, he shall be called the least in the kingdom of heaven: but whosoever shall do and teach them, the same shall be called great in the kingdom of heaven.

—Matthew 5:19

And this is life eternal, that they might know thee the only true God, and Jesus Christ, whom thou hast sent.

—John 17:3

The Gospel s a book of commandments of Jesus of Nazareth with instructions for us to obey the will of His Father, resolve to be partakers in the nature of His Father and participants in our own creation by entering into His Kingdom of God. The Gospel is Good News if one can obey all its divine laws as to inherit eternal life and participate in the glory that Jesus pledged for us. Jesus insisted repeatedly that the obedience of God's law and commandments leads to everlasting life.

The three ABC essential of eternal life, when executed, initiates the earthly phase of the life of Christ in human souls as it strives to gain permanent status of that life after death. The knowledge of the new God, the Father-His will and that one promise of His for mankind, and the great works that Jesus did for His Father, is very important if we are to understand what eternal life is. If mankind can use that knowledge to seek Jesus's kingdom of God as we embark on the creative evolutionary journey that passes through death and resurrection unto that life, then the meaning of human life would reveal itself. The dead people, who lived on this planet and died without this knowledge, will be given the opportunity as promised by Christ, to have this knowledge and if they are willing, will be endowed in the Kingdom of the dead with the Spirit of Christ as to move on to eternal life. The will of His Father and that one promise of the Father for mankind is eternal life through Jesus Christ. "And this is the will of him that sent me, that every one which seeth the Son, and believeth in him, may have everlasting life: and I will raise him up at the last day." (John 6:40)

Jesus Christ was given the authority and power over both the living and the dead-where ever they are-and in heaven and on earth, to give eternal life. "All power is given to me in heaven and on earth." (Matthew 28:18) Yet, in the execution of His task for His Father and mankind Jesus showed profound humility. Jesus maintained this humility as to be able to complete His work. Have you ever read of a humbled God that people worship? Although Jesus was humble, He was very ambitious as was never seen before in the history of the world. Jesus's grand ambition is for all mankind, in all nations of the world, to be endowed with His Spirit-to spiritualize all mankind-and gather them together in one fold under His authority and that of His Father.

The natural history of humanity before and after the death of Jesus Christ remained the same. Many are born, death persists. What is the reason for this unchangeable pattern of human life? The answer is simple: the Father's business-the creation of humans, protecting them and blessing them with eternal life-is still an on-going process. Nothing can impede that evolutionary process until the end of time as determined by the Father. The mystery of eternal life is a deep spirituality. Those who will find the intrinsic meaning of eternal life and be permitted to have a glimpse into that inscrutable mystery, are those who are prepared to be sacrificed because of the purity of their hearts and have, without looking back, embarked on our colossal tasks in the Father's business. They do not take money from people to pray for them or sell bottled holy waters. They are the merciful, compassionate lovers of humanity. Christ belongs to them. The Father belongs to them. The angels call them their brothers and sisters for one single reason: they obey the will of God and believe in Jesus Christ, and have embarked on this creative journey with Christ to meet with them. The preparation for eternal life starts in this world with Jesus's Kingdom of God that came. Use that kingdom of God-the Spirit of Christ- that is within you to:

Promote world peace and justice and use tolerance and negotiations instead of war to accomplish objectives that benefit mankind.

Adopt the principle of never take from poor nations or from the poor in their country, even though you have the opportunity to do so.

Help the poor, educate them, provide adequate health services, and alleviate their sufferings

Avoid hypocrisy and greed, envy, worship of idols, racism, and discrimination.

Seek the truth of the Father that Jesus revealed

Develop expressions of a pure heart and worship the Father in truth.

Have knowledge of the Father and Jesus Christ and use it to work for humanity.

Believe in Jesus Christ and His Father's creative plan for humanity.

Love all that the Lord created and be a servant to humanity and to God the Father

Then wait for your going home! Jesus is waiting for you to come home and be a member of the divine trinity. How can you miss this ultimate union of with the Spirits, rooted in the Spirit of the Father in Christ, epitomized and perfected in the earthly life of Jesus Christ? Nobody, who is willing, is excluded. Jesus opened the door to this life to the poor and the rich, the just and the unjust, the great and small, the old and young, and people of all nations, if they are willing. Even the children of the lesser Gods, who are willing, will become the children of the merciful, forgiving Father; the only God revealed by Jesus Christ and be partakers in the divine nature and glory.

Grace and peace be multiplied unto you through the knowledge of God, and of Jesus our Lord. According as his divine power hath

given unto us all things that pertain unto life and godliness, through the knowledge of him that hath called us to glory and virtue. Whereby are given unto us exceeding great and precious promises: that by these ye might be partakers of the divine nature, having escaped the corruption that is in the world through lust.

—2 Peter 1: 2-4

In His last days, Jesus stood up and cried, saying, "If any man thirst *for the eternal life* let him come unto me....." (John 7:37) The Spirit of the risen Jesus Christ says:

Learn of Me
Take my yoke-my Spirit-on you
Talk to Me
Think of Me
Dream of Me
Run to Me
Seek that one promise of my Father
Participate in your own creation
Come and inherit eternal life!

Temple sacrifices are not needed for eternal life. Long hours of prayers in the temple are not needed for saving and protecting human souls. The sacraments are not needed for eternal life. The sacrifice of a lamb without blemish in the temple to gain atonement is not needed for eternal life. Observation of Jewish temple laws or the Christian human doctrines and dogmas is not needed. Eternal life from the Father and Jesus Christ is not for the Christians only but is for all humanity. The Father who makes the sun rise on the evil and on the good and sends rain on the just and the unjust bestows this gift of His Spirit to all who are ready to receive it. What is needed is for us to inherit eternal life, participate in the earthly stages of the creative process that Jesus revealed in His epic miracle of human creation by the obedience of the will of the Father and the commandments of Christ.

For I have not spoken of myself; but the Father which sent me, he gave me a commandment, what I should say, and what I should speak. And I know that his commandment is life everlasting: whatsoever I speak therefore, even as the Father said unto me, so I speak.

—John 12:49-50

CHAPTER 5

FUTURE ETERNAL LIFE

*If I have told you earthly things, and ye believe not, how
shall ye believe, if I tell you of heavenly things? And no
man hath ascended up to heaven, but He that came down
from heaven, even the Son of man which is in heaven.*

—John 3:12-13

Today you will be with me in Paradise.

—Jesus said to the thief crucified on His right hand

Jesus's eternal life as proclaimed and demonstrated by His
earthly lifestyle and His life after resurrection, showed that it
is present now in human souls, then continues into the future after death. It passes through a trajectory propelled and sustained
by the power of Jesus's kingdom of God to a realized promise of
His Father as demonstrated by Jesus in His miracle of life. Jesus
used Himself as a model. This evolutionary process of the eternal
life in human soul, which was created out of the infinite love of
God, the Father of Christ, the Creator, catapulted the human soul
who inherited it by entering into Jesus's Kingdom of God, to an

everlasting existence in the spiritual world that is beyond human conception and to infinite union with the Father and Jesus Christ. This is what I call the new Trinity of the human spirit: divine bondage of the Father, Jesus Christ and the created human spirit with the life of Christ that originated from the Father. Jesus knew what would be the final reward for all who had forsaken everything and had followed Him: "that they all may be one; as thou, Father art in me, and I in thee, that they also may be one in us, that the world may believe that thou hast sent me." (John 17:21) That was part of Jesus's prayer to His Father for the apostles. However, revealed in that prayer is what awaits all humanity. The divine Trinity of the human soul was echoed by one of His apostles: "That which we have seen and heard, declare us unto you, that ye also may have fellowship with us; and truly our fellowship is with the Father, and with His Son Jesus Christ." (1 John 1:3)

This is the story of the terrestrial and extraterrestrial journey of the human soul with eternal life. Both the eternal life in human souls on earth and in heaven after death is bound together and cannot be broken. The nature is the same. The only difference is that the earthly phase of eternal life is bound with the physical body. The eternal life after death is bound with spiritual body but still endowed with earthly human senses-sight, hearing, touch, taste, memory, affection-as demonstrated by Christ after His resurrection. Eternal life originated from the Spirit of the Father. In essence, the God of Christ is within us. It is a gift to us through Christ for those who have entered into His Kingdom of God.

If ye then be risen with Christ, seek those things which are above, where Christ sitteth on the right hand of God. Set your affection on things above, not on things on the earth. For ye are dead, and your life is hid with Christ in God. When Christ, who is our life, shall appear, then shall ye also appear with him in glory.

—Colossians 3:1-4

This is the life that Jesus came to give to all who are willing to receive it. It is the most important thing in our existence. To create mankind is one thing, to give life to the created mankind is another. Jesus said that it is with us. It is a vital component of Jesus's Kingdom of God. All we have to do is to activate it and inherit the eternal component of that Kingdom. Earthly human existence without that life is not a life. The future of our eternal life after death depends on our possession of that eternal life before death.

> *But ye are not in the flesh, but in the Spirit, if so be that the Spirit of God dwell in you. Now if any man have not the Spirit of Christ, he is none of His. But if the Spirit of him that raised up Jesus from the dead dwell in you, He that raised up Christ from the dead shall also quicken your mortal bodies by His Spirit that dwelleth in you.*

—Romans 8:9, 11

I have always considered the thief who was crucified at the right hand of Christ to be the luckiest man who walked on this planet. He was at the right place and at the right time. He did not enter into Jesus's Kingdom of God before the event that exposed him to Christ. However, he found himself at the grand station with the Master, who was setting it up at Golgotha. It was the greatest of all miracles of all ages that he went with the Master to the Father. "Today you will be with me in Paradise," Jesus said to him as both of them hung on their respective crosses. It was a rare event that never happened and never will again. With God, all things are possible. The only earthly human being who accompanied Jesus to the gate of the Father's kingdom was the blessed thief. The only time in the ministry of Jesus Christ that He promised instantaneous Paradise to anyone was at Golgotha. That promise was also an illustration of a part of why Jesus came to earth: "For the Son of man came to save that which was lost." (Matthew 18:11) It was a demonstration of Jesus's power of bequeathing eternal to whomsoever He wanted. When Jesus united with the Father, He had no money with Him, no silver or gold, no earthly treasures to present to the Father. However, what Jesus presented to the Father was the best of His earthly reward for His victory at Golgotha: the blessed thief. If there was a victory parade in heaven when Jesus returned (I believe there was one), I have no doubt that blessed thief rode beside Him.

When revealed, the inscrutable mystery of the great illustration of the thief who was promised Paradise showed the thief was the first human to ascend to heave, the place Jesus called Paradise. Before that event Jesus had said that, "no man hath ascended up to heaven, but He that came down from heaven, even the Son of man which is in heaven." For the apostles, they had to work and complete the assignment given to them before joining Him in Paradise. Jesus had prayed to His Father; "Father, I will that they also, whom thou hast given me, be with me where I am; that they may behold my glory, which thou hast given me: for thou love me before the foundation of the world." (John 17:24) The blessed thief saw that Paradise and the glory of Christ before the apostles! The event authenticated Jesus's words on the nature of His Father in heaven "who makes His sun to rise on the evil and on the good, and sends rain on the just and on the unjust." (Matthew 5:45) However, the blessed thief provided us with vital information on how to enter into Jesus's Kingdom of God and inherit eternal life before his death. We must use the spiritual tools used by the thief: contempt for injustice, sympathy for the oppressed, repentance, fear and respect for the Father, and the belief in Christ to save him.

The story of the blessed thief was a demonstration of Jesus's power and divine authority to give eternal life to whomsoever He wanted. It was not necessary for Jesus to be crucified and die as to bestow that gift to the blessed thief. "I am come that they might have life and that they might have it more abundantly." (John

10:10) This life is the everlasting life. The glory awaits all humanity. It is God's divine purpose for all humans.

The future of mankind, held in secret- since the first reproductive phase of our creation-was revealed with Jesus's miracle of the earthly stages of human creation. Jesus introduced a new concept- not of the immortality of the soul-but of the nature and destiny of the resurrected human souls. He expanded it to a place where all the resurrected soul will have His Spirit and be with Him and His Father. We were never in that place before. If we make it, nobody will drive you out, except to go on a mission like the apostles who Jesus said "are not of this world." If you want to be a participant in that real future of mankind and have eternal life, that future is in your hand. Jesus proclaimed, prescribed and gave a practical demonstration of everything that is involved in the journey of the human soul to its everlasting glory as to assure you that it is achievable.

And I give unto them eternal life; and they shall never perish; neither shall any man pluck them out of my hand. My Father, which gave them me, is greater than all; and no man is able to pluck them out of my Father's hand. I and my Father are one.

—John 10:28-30

The final destiny of humans is the abode where angels reside: the Paradise. What I have portrayed in this treatise is the journey of the human souls to that Paradise. It is not a journey that goes through hell and purgatory. It a journey that may stop in the kingdom of the dead after resurrection to hear again the words of life from Christ and participate in all activities as I have outlined in the ABC's of eternal life. If they are willing, they will seek first Jesus's Kingdom of God and its righteousness as to gain that spiritual life and then move on. The earthly phase of creating spiritual human beings with the spirit of Christ would come to an end. The earth would no longer be needed as a habitat for humans in their creative spiritual evolution to a divine imagery. Gods' design for humans has nothing to do with the establishment of any type of earthly Kingdom or heavenly Jerusalem. The Father has no plan for eschatological community on this planet that will be ruled by Christ when He descends from the clouds as the Messiah with the twelve apostles and the angels. The human conception of Jesus's Kingdom of God as a place on this planet on earth where everything would be spiritual is a great hindrance to the understanding of that Kingdom and where we are going.

During His transfiguration, Jesus revealed Moses and Elias. (Matthew 17: 1-6) Both Moses and Elias were born like us. Moses never saw or heard the voice of Christ or His Father before he died. The objective of transfiguration was also to reveal resurrected souls-Moses and Elias-who are well known to the Jews. The revealed spiritual images of Moses and Elias provided indisputable evidence of life after death. It was reported in the Gospel that Christ said, "Moses wrote about me." (John 5:46) The truth is that, in his earthly life, Moses never heard of Christ or wrote about Him in the Old Testament literature. There is no text in that book, written by Moses in that book that referred to Christ. It is possible that in the attempt to integrate Judaism with Christianity introduced by Christ, books surfaced that bore the information that Moses wrote about Christ. However, the spirit of Moses after his resurrection saw Christ, before Jesus was sent to this world by His Father. Perhaps, this vital information if revealed to the Jews would interfere with the trajectory of the works of Jesus, and hence the instruction: "Tell the vision to no man, until the Son of man be risen from the dead."

If you have been reading this book from the beginning, you already know whom you are and why we are all here on this planet. I have made many references in this treatise that God is still creating us, and that this earthly phase is just a single phase in the creative cycle. This plan was in place before Abraham was born. Adam and

Eve underwent the same process we are experiencing now. From the beginning of time, all humans, regardless of race, nationality, or social status, have had to pass through the three earthly stages of human creation. We are conceived the same way and for this reason: "at the beginning, God made them males and females." (Matthew 19:4) We will, if you are willing, complete this earthly phase of human creation the same way, by death, and move on to the next spiritual phase. This cycle is irrepressible. The duration of this phase is hidden from humans. It could last from a few seconds or few days for some people. It could last for years. Some human spirits may be given a second chance in the Kingdom of the dead and some may be sent back to this phase to repeat the cycle. In the final spiritual phase, there are no marriages. "The children of this world marry, and are given in marriage. But they which shall be accounted worthy to obtain that world, and the resurrection from the dead, neither marry nor are given in marriage; neither can they die anymore; for they are equal unto the angels; and are the children of God, being the children of the resurrection." (Luke 20:34-36) There are no million-dollar mansions, no run-down homes, no gold or silver because everything is left behind. It is for this reason that Jesus said: "sell everything, give to the poor and follow Me." The quest for the accumulation of earthly treasures forms an impassable barrier to the comprehension and execution of what Christ prescribed and demonstrated for eternal life. Death is a grand station along the pathway of our creation. Of what use are all the earthly treasures-especially if accumulated by taking advantage of the poor or by taking away the natural resources of the poor nations without helping them-to us who must die?

For what shall it profit a man, if he shall gain the whole world, and lose his own soul.

—Mark. 8:36

Verily, verily, I say unto you, He that heareth my word, and believeth on him that sent me, hath everlasting life, and shall not come into condemnation; but is passed from death unto life.

—John 5:24

Do not take your last breath on this Earth without having entered into Jesus's Kingdom of God, inheriting eternal life, experiencing it and manifested that experience to the world. That is the password to pass from death into the future life. Paul's ambition was to present us to the Father, at the time of our departure from this world with activated Jesus's Kingdom of God within us.

Even the mystery which hath been hid from ages and from generations, but now is made manifest to his saints: To whom God would make known what is the riches of the glory of this mystery among the Gentiles; which is Christ in you, the hope of glory: Whom we preach, warning every man, and teaching every man in all wisdom; that we may present every man perfect in Christ Jesus: Whereunto I also labor, striving according to his working, which worketh in me mightily.

—Colossians 1:26-29

He that hath the Son hath life; and he that hath not the Son of God hath not life.

—1 John 5:12

The eternal life for those who posses it in this world continue to have that life forever after death. That life is an essential divine attribute of the Spirit of the Father they inherited through Christ by entering into His Kingdom of God.

The Master is come, and calleth for thee.

—John 11:28

Today, the Master, Jesus Christ is still calling us to follow Him, learn how to receive the gift (the Spirit of His Father) from Him. If you do not have the earthy phase of eternal life, you will have no life at all. Without your possession of this life that is in the Spirit of the Father, you will not be a participant in the earthly stages of your own creation as demonstrated by Jesus Christ in His epic miracle of human creation. In essence, eternal life is placed in a strategic position in the human creative trajectory in the earthly stages of the transcendental transformation of the human soul as it strives to be fully created. It continues with that life forever after death. Jesus came to give us the creative element in the Spirit of His Father, and give it to us abundantly that we may have life.

CHAPTER 6

JESUS'S ROLE IN HUMAN CREATION

For by him were all things created, that are in heaven, and that are in earth, visible and invisible, whether they be thrones, or dominions, or principalities, or powers: all things were created by him, and for him.

—Colossians 1:16

In the beginning was the Word, and the Word was with God, and the Word was (a) God. The same was in the beginning with God. All things were made by Him; and without Him was not anything made that was made.

—John 1:1-3

My Lord, my God! -

—Apostle Thomas

We believe in one God, the Father, the Almighty, of all that is, seen and unseen. We believe in one Lord, Jesus Christ,

> *the only begotten of the Father, God from God, Light*
> *from Light, true God from true God,..........* Text from
> Nicene Creed

All the above references indicated that Jesus is a God and a Creator. However the authors did not give us any convincing evidence to support their assertions. Jesus complicated the issue by saying that, "I and my Father are One." (John 10:30) The Jews perceived and rightfully so, that Jesus was projecting Himself as a God and took up stones to stone Him. (John 10:31-33) My aim in this epiphany is to give you a step by step guide with evidence as proclaimed and demonstrated by Christ that He is also a Creator and a God that creates and controls human life with His Father. It is my hope that this systemic patterned presentation will fortify your belief in words and works of Christ.

> *Verily, verily, I say unto you, The Son can do nothing of himself,*
> *but what he seeth the Father do: for what things soever he doeth,*
> *these also doeth the Son likewise. For the Father loved the Son, and*
> *showed him all things that himself doeth: and he will show him*
> *greater works than these that ye may marvel.*

> —John 5:19-20

The greater work, the demonstration of the everlasting monumental deed-human creation-Jesus learned from the Father is the subject of this epiphany. It was a demonstration of who are the Gods creating human beings. The Father and Jesus Christ have been creating human beings from the very beginning. However, the greater works Jesus did that you may marvel was His everlasting miracle of earthly stages of human creation. Jesus used Himself as the model. It was the first time ever such an epic miracle was successfully executed, not in heaven or on this planet Earth.

If I do not the works my Father does, believe me not. But if I do, though ye believe not me, believe the works: that ye may know, and believe, that the Father is in me, and I in him.

—John 10:37-39

The Father's business as reported in the true Gospel of Christ is all about earthly stages of human creation. Jesus came to demonstrate that work and to reveal to reveal His Father, who also works on a Sabbath day as the only true Creator God of human. In doing so, Jesus also revealed Himself as a Creator. However, Jesus did not hide the fact that He gained the knowledge of human creation from His Father.

Verily, verily, I say unto you, The Son can do nothing of himself, but what he seeth the Father do: for what things soever he doeth, these also doeth the Son likewise. For the Father loved the Son, and showed him all things that himself doeth: and he will show him greater works than these that ye may marvel. For as the Father raiseth up the dead, and quickeneth them; even so the Son quickeneth whom He will.

—John 5:19-21

In the transcendental transformation of the human soul in its creative evolution as it seeks to be fully created as was demonstrated by Jesus's epic miracle of life, the power of His Kingdom of God, the creative element of eternal life in that Kingdom played significant role in that process. Death and resurrection are all positioned on the creative trajectory of the human soul in its journey gain full expression as spiritual being. In my attempt to reveal Jesus's role in human creation, I have forayed into deeper mysteries of epic demonstration of Jesus's staged demonstration of the everlasting miracle of human creation. Jesus used Himself as the model that revealed Him as divine authority who controls life and resurrection. This authority was given to Him by His Father. With this vital information you do not need to need to be a trained cryptologist as to decode the sayings of Jesus in these His encrypted utterances.

I am the Bread of Life.

—John 6:48

I am the Resurrection and the Life.

—John 6:25

I am the Way, the Truth and the Life.

—John 14:6

"I and my Father are One."

—(John 10:30)

I came that they might have life, and that they might have it abundantly.

—John 10:10

Jesus Christ was born into this world as a human being. If Jesus was able to recreate Himself and controlled the death, the resurrection and the eternal life during that process, then the search for who is creating mankind is over. By using Himself in His epic miracle of the earthly stages of human creation, Jesus revealed Himself as Creator of human beings Jesus demonstrated what His Father taught Him. Human beings have lived on this planet Earth for many years before Jesus came. All those years, Jesus Christ and His Father remain hidden. The momentous questions are: what then prompted the Father to send Jesus Christ to the world to reveal Him? Who is this Father and who is Jesus Christ? What is their business with us? Do they have businesses in other parts of the Universe?

What Jesus accomplished showed that we are not isolated from one another. I have persistently again and again, directed attention to the earthly work of Jesus in human creation as was portrayed in His epic miracle of human creation. That miracle also revealed something amazing and startling that is not found in any other religion: that human beings do participate in the earthly phase of their creation. The transcendental transformation of mankind to full expression as spirits would not be possible if we refuse to participate in our creation. The road to Paradise would be closed if we fail to participate. In essence, Jesus's epic miracle of human creation also revealed the creative power in the human soul. The creative power of the human soul is not the power to create other people. It is the power given to you when you enter into Jesus's Kingdom of God. How you use the creative power is what you get in the end. To use it well, leads to eternal life. To refuse or abuse it is to reject His offer of eternal life and be not created at all.

To explore the role of Jesus in creation is to sail into the sea of infinite mysteries. For indeed it is the mystery of all mysteries that reveals why He came, what He was doing with the Spirit of the Father in Him and why it was necessary to demonstrate to the world what He was doing with His Father for mankind before He came to this world. It is the basket that holds the mysteries of:

Why Jesus was sent by His Father
His Father's will for Him
His task from His Father for mankind
Eternal life
The creative power of the Spirit of His Father in Him

What He and His Father have been doing with human life
before Jesus came
The infinite power of His Kingdom of God
Why He died and resurrected Himself
The earthly stages of human creation
The creative power in human souls
Who Jesus and His Father are
Who are we and why we are here

From the beginning to the end, reappearing persistently in the true Gospel of Christ, the Acts of the Apostles, the letters of Paul, Jesus's proclamations on what He planned to do, although no one comprehended it and the demonstration of His role in human creation were the major events that brought Jesus to the world. In the execution of those events, Jesus Christ and His Father were for the first time, revealed to the world as Creators.

> *Unto me, who am less than the least of all saints, is this grace given, that I should preach among the Gentiles the unsearchable riches of Christ; And to make all men see what is the fellowship of the mystery, which from the beginning of the world hath been hid in God, who created all things by Jesus Christ*

—Ephesians 3:8-9

Paul's "unsearchable riches of Christ" points to the trajectory of Jesus's role in human creation.

> *For by him were all things created, that are in heaven, and that are in earth, visible and invisible, whether they be thrones, or dominions, or principalities, or powers: all things were created by him, and for him.*

—Colossians 1:16

The *modus operandi* of the unsearchable riches of Christ in human creation remains hidden for the last two thousand years, and yet they are scattered everywhere in the true Gospel of Christ. My responsibility is to reveal to the public what I recovered from the Gospel on *the modus operandi* of the unsearchable riches of Christ in human creation, that humankind may have a glimpse into the mystery of His role in creation. The mysteries of the death and resurrection that in the past were inscrutable and unsearchable are now searchable and revealed. The mysteries point to one direction only: Jesus's role in human creation and the revelation of His Father.

All things are delivered to me of my Father: and no man knoweth who the Son is, but the Father; and who the Father is, but the Son, and he to whom the Son will reveal him.

—Jesus. Luke 10:22

The wonderful story of Jesus Christ and the instructions that He got from His Father for mankind, was an epic demonstration of the journey of the ship of His Christianity as it sails on the river of the living water, carrying along with it, the human souls to the final destiny. It is still going on today. It was an exhibition that revealed God, His Father as the Creator and Himself also a Creator. Jesus was given the power and authority to demonstrate to us what they have been doing since the beginning of the earthly stages of human creation. The comprehension of Jesus's Kingdom of God and His role of Jesus in the earthly phase of human creation using Himself as an example are the hermeneutic keys to the knowledge of who Jesus is, the authority and power of His Father, who we are, why we are here, and where we are going.

Jesus, as a human being, with the Spirit of His Father in Him-the spiritualization of Jesus with Spirit of the Father-supported His utterance that He has the spiritual life that is in His Father. "For as the Father hath life in himself; so hath he given to the Son to have life in Himself." (John 5:26) This is the mystery of Jesus's saying: "I am in the Father and the Father in Me." (John 14:10) Mankind got the Spirit of the Father through Christ

Jesus, already spiritualized with the Spirit of His Father, gave a once upon a time demonstration of the acts of the earthly stages of human creation and revealed them with a creative trajectory of multiple platforms.

His Death at Golgotha
His Resurrection
Revelation of the prototype of the created spiritual mankind showcased in His resurrected image

The spiritualization of the apostles and the seventy men He sent out to cities and villages in Palestine, His glorified risen Spirit given to the apostles on the day of Pentecost, His promise of giving the same Spirit of the Father to everyone, if we are willing to receive it, revealed that we have what are required to be fully created as was showcased in His resurrected image. Death and resurrection are positioned along the human creative trajectory. The new paradigm of creation under the above evolutional creative human platforms was used by Jesus in the demonstration of what He and His Father were doing, even before He came to this world. Jesus used Himself as a model to give a practical demonstration of how they are creating us. All other roads to the journey of the human soul to its destiny are closed. The game is over if you are looking for who is Jesus and the Father that He revealed to the world. All avenues for further exploration for more information on that subject are closed. It is no longer necessary to go to Jerusalem to look for the bones of Jesus or for archeological evidence for what happened at Golgotha. It is no longer necessary to look for historical Jesus. You will find all that you are looking for in Jesus's miracle of human creation and in His Kingdom of God.

Mankind, when fully created, are spiritual beings as Jesus demonstrated on the day of His resurrection. Jesus gave a practiced demonstration of the earthly phase of creative process using His power of the Spirit of the Father in Him. This illuminated the spiritual aspect of the creative process. The story on creation in this epiphany is not rumination on creation as portrayed by the book of Genesis. Fundamentally, it is a different story of the earthly phases of creation-the spiritual phase-that starts at birth and continues through death and resurrection. It is the story of the concept of the earthly phase human creation, hidden from mankind but revealed to us by Christ.

Therefore doth my Father love me, because I lay down my life, that I might take it again. No man takes it from me, but I lay it down of myself. I have power to lay it down, and I have power to take it again. This commandment have I received of my Father.

—John 10:17-18

Jesus resurrected Himself. He has the ability to resurrect. "And this is the will of Him that sent me; that everyone which seeth the Son and believeth on Him, may have everlasting life; and I will raise him up at the last day, (John 6:40) Jesus came to this world as a human being. By the power of His kingdom of God and His ability to recreate Himself by resurrection to a spiritual form, Jesus's power of human creation was made manifest. This is the mystery of Golgotha. You will notice that in the demonstration of this infinite mystery of creation, His Father did not lift a finger to help Him. Jesus did all of it by Himself. Jesus had to report to the Father before Mary Magdalene could touch Him. The entire process was executed with precisions. That was the Good News. Unfortunately that great exhibition was misinterpreted by many people.

Jesus came to this world as a human being and left as a spiritual being: the risen Christ. His life did not start in this world and did not end here. His epic demonstration showed that we as human beings can leave this world as spiritual beings. To understand this epiphany of Jesus' role in creation in the transformation of a human being to a spiritual being, you must look at Jesus Christ as a human being. Jesus came down from heaven, born into this world as a human being with the Spirit of His Father. It is this Spirit of the Father that He gave freely to everyone on this planet. Jesus presented Himself like us, gave us the same gift, the Spirit He got from His Father, for this simple reason: to learn from Him, witness the creative process, participate in the process and leave this planet as a divine beings.

Earthly life is unfinished life. To understand the earthly stages of creation, Jesus did it by recreating Himself. This will give you the answer to that perplexing question: Why are we here? The answer, as I have been categorically presenting in this entire treatise is to evolve from our human nature to a divine nature. Jesus gave a practical demonstration of all the processes that are involved and equipped us with the core element-the Spirit of the Father- we need. The only way to convince you, not only to believe in what Jesus did, but also to encourage you to participate in this creative process of real human life, is to reveal this mystery of all the mysteries-the mystery of earthly stages of human creation as demonstrated by Christ-is and to take you step by step from one mystery of the everlasting miracle to another until we get to root of the role of Jesus in the earthly phase of human creation and what it means to all mankind in this 21st century

Perhaps, when we have this knowledge, we will stop killing each other, knowing well that if we do, we are killing what God, the Father and Jesus Christ are creating. With this knowledge, the uncertainty of who we are and why we are here vanishes. The earth will be made up of borderless nations and there will be no more wars and refugee camps. We will all reach out to one another as brothers and sisters. We will love one another. Hatred and jealousy will vanish. Arsenals of nuclear weaponry will be never be used. But this utopia is definitely possible if we are willing to participate in our creation and believe in what Jesus proclaimed and demonstrated.

The Father sent Jesus to the world as a human being in order to demonstrate the model process for the earthly phase of the creative process and its ultimate end. The big question is this: how could a human being be involved in the creation of mankind? This idea is unimaginable if you still do not know that you are involved in the creative process. You are not in this world as a spectator, standing immobilized, waiting for Jesus and His Father to complete the earthy phase of your creation. You are actively involved in it, if you are willing. The Father and Jesus Christ are involved and they are willing to transform us to new creatures-spiritual beings-by what was demonstrated by Jesus in His epic miracle of human creation. To accept what was showcased at the end of that miracle as a prototype of spiritual mankind, is to acknowledge that Jesus Christ is a Creator and also a God on the ground that only a God can create humans. The Jews had always accused Jesus of portraying Himself a God. Jesus never denied it.

I and the Father are One.

—Jesus

Today, to believe that Jesus, who came as a human being-humiliated, crucified, died and risen from the dead, played a role in our creation is beyond the possibility of any understanding. This divine transformation of our nature by Jesus Christ is difficult to comprehend, if we persistently proclaim that the metaphysical drama at Golgotha where Jesus was crucified was a sacrifice and atonement required by His Father for all our sins, including the original sins we inherited from Adam and Eve. The mystery of Golgotha will remain hidden if we continue to look at it as events that brought salvation. It would be an unacceptable exposition to all who credited human creation to the God revealed by Moses in the book of Genesis. It will persistently be an inscrutable mystery if we continue to look at the words and works of Christ with the lens of Immaculate Conception of Jesus and with the Hubble Telescopes of Trinity. The concept of Trinity, introduced the Holy Ghost as a separate God. The Holy Ghost is the glorified Spirit of the risen Christ. The Father first sent Jesus as a human being for what Jesus accomplished at Golgotha. Subsequently after His resurrection and ascension, the glorified Spirit of the risen Christ was sent down again by His Father for the continuation of the Father's business to its glorious end. With the elimination of the concept of Trinity, what happened to the apostles on the day of Pentecost became the light that illuminates the role of Christ in human creation and the power of His Kingdom of God when viewed with the lens of His death and resurrection.

Today, many people have challenged the report of creation as revealed in the book of Genesis by Moses. I also do not believe in this particular version of the creation story. I do not believe that Adam and Eve were created in a Paradise or that the history of mankind originated from them. To accept the concept that Adam and Eve were the first created human beings is to accept that the history of mankind originated from the Jewish history. I do not believe in the sins of Adam and Eve that prompted the Jewish God to expel them. The nature of that sin has eluded mankind. I believe in what Jesus Christ said: *"that we are from here."* We are from this planet, born of water [not by water baptism] and that we must be born again of the Spirit. If we remove from our consciousness the story of Adam and Eve and the concept of original sin, we must redefine and reform our current explanations on why Jesus died as well as our concept of salvation. Christian theologians and the Church are preoccupied with trying to present Jesus Christ as the Messiah, the Son of God, who sits at the right hand of God, the Redeemer, and Savior of mankind from sins. We are encouraged to find Christ in sacraments and inherit eternal life by eating the bread and drinking the wine offered at Eucharist. This epiphany on His role in human creation opens the spiritual door for you to look at Jesus Christ and behold His glory in the vast Paradise of His Father's Kingdom in your hearts. To believe in His Father and in Jesus Christ whom He sent and in His words and works is to have this privilege. Why wait? Grasp it now. Jesus said that it is your Father's good pleasure it to you.

This subtitle may offend some people on the ground that creation in any form is God's prerogative and solely in His power. Jesus never claimed to be His Father.

"The Father is greater than I"

However, what Jesus claimed is that His Father gave Him all authorities and power in heaven and on earth and that the spirit of the Father in Him was doing the works that included the earthly phase of human creation. Mankind missed this vital knowledge on the practical demonstration of the earthly phase of the creative process of mankind and His role in making it happen. Jesus used Himself as a model. Jesus controlled what He came to do. What He accomplished made Him and His Father Lords of creation. It is in this role in creativity that you will find Jesus's divinity and His power.

> *Through him all things were made; without him nothing was made that has been made. In Him was life, and the life was the light of men.*
>
> —John 1:3-4

Jesus Christ suffered, humbled Himself to become human as to give us a practical demonstration of our earthly life as a journey of human creation. Jesus made Himself a hybrid of human creation. What Jesus demonstrated is still going on today. All aspects of the earthly stages of human creation were controlled by Jesus as authorized by His Father. Jesus allowed Himself to participate in all that is human in order to demonstrate by His epic miracle of human creation-the creative pathway of humans to a greater glory. He used Himself as an example. It was the *modus operandi* of revealing Himself in human creation.

The role of Jesus in creation-as demonstrated by Him in words and works-has its own intrinsic meaning. To explore that Father-Jesus Christ-human creative trajectory of the human soul is to explore the infinite mystery that originated from God, His Father that revealed Jesus, not only as a Creator but also as a God with creative power and authority of all things in heaven and earth, given to Him by His Father.

All power is given unto me in heaven and in earth.

—Jesus. Matthew 28: 18

All things are delivered unto me of my Father.

—Matthew 11:27

The Father loved the Son, and hath given all things into His hand.

—John 3:3

The conception of Jesus Christ as a Creator of mankind, requires us to rethink and reexamine the traditional ways of understanding Jesus' Kingdom of God, eternal life, His death, and His resurrection. It requires us to reexamine our current understanding of creation as presented in the book of Genesis by Moses. The very core of the Good News to mankind is this Jesus's creative work, that opens the portals of heavenly things for mankind, and for the first time in its history, mankind touched and spoke to a spirit:

the Spirit of the risen Christ. There is no record that Founders of other religions ever reappeared in a spiritual form that many people saw, touched and communicated openly with that spirit. This is again a special feature that differentiated the new Christianity of Christ from other religions of this world. If we are to understand this link that connects all mankind, we as Christians must reform our understanding-as presented to us-of the imagery of salvation as a purchase by the blood and death of Jesus as ransom for original sin. All of these gross misunderstandings have alienated Christians from people of other religions. It created divisions even among Christians. Many of our pre-conceived ideas antagonized and confused people-including our children.

The role of Christ in human creation and all its intrinsic meanings can be captured by a deeper exploration of the infinite mysteries of Jesus's Kingdom of God, His death resurrection as demonstrated in His once upon a time epic miracle of human creation.

(1) The Infinite Mystery of Jesus's Kingdom of God

The Spirit of Christ in human souls as the Kingdom of God in action takes a strategic position in the earthly phase of human creation. The formula that I used and have been presenting in the entire epistemology of what I recovered from the true Gospel of Christ is that there is only one gift from His Father to mankind, for His one purpose for us. That blessing is the gift of His Spirit through Jesus Christ for the initiation and promulgation of the earthly phase of human creation. Without the gift of the Spirit of the Father to mankind through Christ, all creation of the spiritual human being will not be possible. Jesus' Kingdom of God sets a platform of the propitious creative power of Christ through which one can have a glimpse of the creative human life cycle that was set in motion by Jesus. The demonstration was powered by the Spirit of the Father in the human soul of Jesus Christ and set in motion by Jesus Himself.

The story of Jesus' Kingdom of God is the story of the initiation of the earthly phase of human creation, portrayed like a play in a theater. This story portrays what God and Jesus Christ were doing before Jesus came to the world, what Jesus came to do, what they are still doing today, and what they will continue to do in the future. The greatest mission the world ever witnessed was indeed a planned showcase of how the Father and Jesus Christ are creating us. The mystery of Jesus' Kingdom of God is the mystery of creation. What started with the proclamation that the kingdom of God was coming by Jesus who demonstrated its presence by performing miracles, evolved to spiritual events beyond our imagination. The mystery of the earthly stages of creation revealed itself with Jesus's possession of the Spirit of His Father. Jesus' ability to spiritualize human souls with that Spirit in essence revealed His divine power and Godly attributes. The Jews believed that only a God revealed to them by Moses, can spiritualize souls and forgive sins. They accused Jesus of falsely claiming to be a God. By the proclamation of Jesus's endowment of His Spirit to human souls, exemplified by Paul's proclamation of *"Christ in me,"* the ground was set for the slaughter of the apostles, Paul, and the early disciples by the Jews as they attempted to disseminate that message.

Jesus had introduced a new dimension of human perception of creation by claiming and then demonstrating His ability to spiritualize-to incarnate-human souls with His Spirit- by the ordination of His apostles with His Spirit. Jesus sent them out to demonstrate the power of that His Kingdom. On another occasion, the same thing happened to the seventy men Jesus sent out, having spiritualized their souls, instructed them to go the cities and villages to showcase the power of the Kingdom that came. Empowered with the Spirit of Christ, they carried out their mission. They were the ones who had a 'taste' of Jesus's Kingdom of God and manifested its power. The story of Jesus' Kingdom of God with all its related parables is the story of creation, projected in a framework of educating the public on this new paradigm of creation, demonstrating the power of what is being created by the apostles' performance of miracles with the power of Jesus' Kingdom of God within them.

The modus operandi used by Jesus in giving His Spirit to human souls remained an inscrutable mystery, even as of today. That Spirit of Jesus Christ in human souls, when explored, reveals His creative activity in the initiation and propagation of the transcendent evolutionary creative process of the human soul to its glorious end. Only a Supreme Being with Godhead attributes could accomplish this transcendental transformation. In essence, Jesus is a Supreme Being with creative power. In the parable of the vine, Jesus also portrayed the Father as the head of creation. (John 15: 1-6) Additionally, Jesus told the Jews that what He was doing He learned them from His Father.

> *Then answered Jesus and said unto them, Verily, verily, I say unto you, The Son can do nothing of himself, but what he seeth the Father do: for what things soever he doeth, these also doeth the Son likewise. For the Father loves the Son, and showed him all things that himself doeth: and he will show him greater works than these that ye may marvel.*

> —John 5:19-20

Unfortunately, neither the Jews nor the apostles asked Jesus to tell them what the great marvelous works were. Christianity of today still does not understand the mighty works. If the Christian leaders understood it, they could have given mankind the concrete, verifiable, documented, demonstrated evidence of the "true God from true God" without any creed. They could have simply educated mankind by the mighty work of Christ that unites all of mankind, regardless of their nationality, race or religion. They could have revealed the meaning of Jesus's Kingdom of God to the world.

Jesus introduced a new God, His Father that is accessible, not in human or animal sacrifices, but in prayers and in our participation in our own creation. Jesus cried out again and again-*"Follow me,"* That plea was not only directed to the apostles and the rich, young rulers, or the lawyers but to all of us to be spectators of the momentous epic miracle of human creation, learn from Him how we can participate in our own creation.

>*"Learn of me"*
>*"Come to me that you may have life,"* Jesus told the Jews.
>*"I am the Porter. No one comes to the Father except through me."*
>*"I am the Shepherd"* that guides you in your journey to eternal
>   life.

Why hate or be jealous of Jesus and His creative power when He also gave you all of the opportunity to be a spirit like Him? Why kill the Messenger who brought the gift for mankind from His Father? Jesus placed Himself-as was the will of the Father-along the human creative pathway, making Himself a Lord in creation, authorized by His Father, to demonstrate the earthly phase of human creation with the power of the Spirit of His Father in Him-the power of the Spirit of the Father in His human soul. This is the mystery of Jesus' Kingdom of God. Jesus was all the time performing miracles with that power. Jesus's everlasting miracle of the earthly stages of human creation, powered by His Kingdom of God, was the grandeur of all His miracles. After the Apostolic age, it was relegated to the background as the Christian leaders sought earthly powers and treasures.

The sources of my epistemology on the role of Jesus in the creation are His words and the epitome of His work and earthly life as recorded in His true Gospel. However, John the Baptist said that, "A man can receive nothing, except it be given to him from Heaven." (John 3:27)

For the full comprehension of the mystery of Jesus' role in creation, we must press on to another mystery within its contents: the mystery of His death.

In reminiscence, Jesus' Kingdom of God is the invisible staircase that transverses all the paths of the earthly phase of human creation. It started with *"Christ in me"* and leads the spiritualized human soul to other grand stages of creation, of which death is one of them. What is revealed in Jesus's Kingdom of God enables one to have a glimpse into the mysteries of the death and resurrection of Jesus. It provided a platform on which one can stand to know Jesus and His Father. It enables the reader not only to have knowledge of who we are, why we are here, but also to look beyond the present visible world and perceive the spiritual bond that binds all human souls together with the Spirits of the Father and Jesus Christ.

Jesus's Kingdom of God is the way and the only way through which all generations, regardless of their nationality, religious background and ethnicity, would develop and advance their intelligence during the preparatory phase on this planet Earth, in their transcendental transformation to a fuller destiny. The works of Jesus would not be possible without the power of the Kingdom of God. Without it, we are nothing. With it, we will have life and have it abundantly.

(11) The Death of Jesus

Jesus said unto them, When ye have lifted up (on the cross) the Son of man, then shall ye know that I am He.

—John 8:28

Something big happened about two thousand years ago at Golgotha, where Jesus Christ died on the cross at a young age. How could it be? Jesus's seven words on the cross gave no indication as to why He had to die at that young age. His Father had remained silent why Jesus had to die. Jesus did not reveal to anyone why He had to die. What does the death of Jesus Christ means to us in the world we live in today? We live in a community with long history of wars, murders, gang-styled drug related executions, political and religious killings and elimination of the enemy by hanging, guillotine or firing squads. We kill to protect our nations. We kill to secure the future of our children. We kill to take control of earthly treasures. We plunder and pillage. We kill to defend our rights. Perhaps, the knowledge of death as demonstrated by Jesus and why Jesus, with all His powers, allowed the Jews to condemn Him to death, crucified by the Romans and died, may bring us to what we may have to reform what we deemed as an impossible task: stop killing human beings, be good to everyone including the enemies and shun the policy of hatred and intolerance. The importance of this knowledge is vital as was revealed in the story of Bernard Fallot by Jean Bobognano in *Quartier des fauves, prison de Fresnes, Edition du Fuseau.* This story was reported by Albert Camus in his *Reflections on the Guillotine*

"*Barnard Fallot of the Masug gang, who worked for the Gestapo, confessed to the entire list of the terrible crimes of which he was accused and later went on to his death with great courage, declaring himself beyond hope of reprieve: "My hands are too red with blood," he said to one of his prisoners. After having declared that he wanted to die bravely, Fallot told the same prisoner: "Do you know what I regret most of all? Not having known sooner about the Bible they gave me here. If I had, I wouldn't be where I am now."*

Perhaps, the late Adolf Hitler of Germany would say the same thing: that he had knowledge of the history of the Spanish Grand Inquisition and Pogroms; that the knowledge of what Christ prescribed, proclaimed and demonstrated at Golgotha were not revealed to him. Jesus and His Father placed death on the trajectory of the journey of the human souls. What human beings have done and are still doing today, is to snatch and steal from Jesus Christ and His Father, the control of death and administer it at their own will. This lack of understanding on the meaning of physical death contributes significantly to today's world's instability.

On His way to Golgotha, Jesus told His sympathizers not to weep for Him. "Daughters of Jerusalem weep not for me..." (Luke 23:28) Jesus knew the reason for such instruction. Why weep when they were on their way to see the greatest show on earth played on the grand station at Golgotha that would complete His earthly task from His Father and for mankind? Why weep when they were following the greatest exhibiter of what was once talked about-the creation of a human being-but no one had ever seen it? Why weep for the spiritual event that would seal with evidence, His role in human creation? Why must they weep for the exhibition of the epic miracle that would reveal His Father as the true God the Creator, who reigns and controls all things? Jesus told His apostles to rejoice because He was going to the Father. "If you love me, you would rejoice, because I am going to the Father, for my Father is greater that I" (John 14:28)

Golgotha was the grand station-the epicenter of the world-along the path of human creation, where Jesus revealed His power to recreate Himself. It was the platform Jesus used to reveal Himself and His Father. The moment Jesus was lifted up on that cross, everything changed. Timing was very important in the execution of Jesus's task from His Father. The crucifixion of Jesus was carried out during the week of the Passover feast. The Father and Jesus Christ wanted the people who came to Jerusalem from many parts of the world to witness that event. The Father and His Son waited until the time was fulfilled.

> *If I do not the works of my Father, believe me not. But if I do, though you believe not me, believe the works; that you may know and believe that the Father is in me, and I in the Father.*

> —John 10:37–38

To follow Jesus to the cross is an invitation not only to be a spectator of that work from His Father but to use that knowledge of the glory of station-death-that the Father and Christ have placed along our creative trajectory. Death is a blessing as demonstrated by Christ and not a curse. The blessings of the human soul as it moves along the path of its creative trajectory with the Spirit of Christ, was not achieved by the death of Christ or by the atonement of our sins as to please the Father. The blessed soul equipped with Jesus's Kingdom of God, is the highest blessing bestowed on mankind by the Father, through Jesus Christ. However, as it journeys to its destiny, it must pass through death. Golgotha was not the place where Jesus conquered death. How can He, who with His Father placed death along the path of creation for all mankind, eliminate what they put along the path of creation even before Jesus came? What Jesus demonstrated at Golgotha was that death was one of the modus operandi used in human creation and that He was a Creator using that *modus operandi* to recreate Himself, This is the mystery of Golgotha. All other roads to human conceived mysteries of Golgotha-ransom, remission of sins, the sting of death, the Blood of the New Testament which was shed for many for forgiveness of sins and for atonement, and defeat of Satan-are closed.

In reminiscence, His death was the *modus operandi*-a creative platform-Jesus used to reveal Himself in creation. Jesus allowed Himself to participate in all that is human as to demonstrate the creative path of mankind. He used Himself as an example. Although it was planned by His Father, every stage of it was controlled by Him. This power and authority over His death was granted to Him by His Father. Jesus's proclamation that "It is finished," just before He died was not an indication that He had completed the show. It was a proclamation that nothing can stop what He came to reveal and to demonstrate: His role in creation by recreating Himself and the revelation of His Father. What is hidden beyond the 'tragedy' of Golgotha exploded into the deepest infinite mystery of the Creator of mankind as the demonstration of the epic miracle of the human creation moves to the final stage: the resurrection of Jesus. When revealed as executed one would begin to understand many of Jesus's words. If you want proof that Jesus is also a Creator of mankind, that His loving merciful Father is the

Father of all mankind and that His Father is a living true God who controls all things, please continue to read this epiphany.

(111) Jesus's Resurrection

I am the Resurrection

—Jesus

As I discussed in the last few pages on death, Jesus is waiting at that grand station on the creative pathway to resurrect you in accordance with His Father's will for mankind.

> *For I came down from heaven, not to do mine own will, but the will of him that sent me. And this is the Father's will which hath sent me, that of all which he hath given me I should lose nothing, but should raise it up again at the last day. And this is the will of him that sent me, that every one which seeth the Son, and believeth in him, may have everlasting life: and I will raise him up at the last day.*

—John 6:38-40

Jesus's task from His Father was also to validate and exemplify that process by resurrecting Himself. "For as the Father has life in Himself, so He granted the Son to have life in Himself." (John 5:26)

Jesus's miracle of recreating Himself through the spiritualization of His soul by His Father with His Spirit and His death was made manifest at His resurrection. The resurrection of Jesus revealed the mysteries of creation by God, the Father who taught Jesus how to resurrect and create spiritual human spirits.

> *Verily, verily, I say unto you, The Son can do nothing of Himself, but what He sees the Father do: for what things soever He does, these also do the Son likewise. For the Father loves the Son, and showed*

*Him all things that Himself do: and He will show Him greater
works than these, that ye may marvel. For as the Father raises up
the dead, and quickens (resurrects) them; even so the Son quickens
whom He will.*

—John 5:19-21

It was the portal through which we see the new God, the Father
that Jesus presented to the world as a Creator and a living God
that exists. It revealed that one gift of the Father-the gift of His
Spirit through Christ-for mankind and the will of the Father for
Jesus: to give mankind a practical demonstration of the earthly
phase of creation using Himself as a hybrid of what He is creating.
It is within this role as a Creator with His Father that the divine
nature and the Godlike attributes of Christ are revealed. This is
the deep mystery of the new Christianity of Christ that was revealed by Jesus's epic miracle of human creation. It is the mystery
that revealed Jesus as a Creator and a God. All other assertions,
assumptions or proclamations in attempts to prove that Jesus is a
Lord and a God are off the track. When the apostle Thomas was
permitted to look into this mystery, all doubts about His Master
dissipated. Mary Magdalene and the apostle Thomas were the only
two people on that day we celebrate as Easter that understood the
significance of divine image of the risen Christ as evidenced by
their joyful proclamations.

Rabboni!

—Mary Magdalene

My Lord, my God!

—Apostle Thomas

Jesus, like nobody before Him or after Him, revealed to mankind who we are: little children with bodies and souls-not created human being driven away from Paradise-undergoing a new creative process under His power and with the gift of the Spirit from His Father, our God and participating in their own creation. Only Gods can create human beings. If Jesus can recreate Himself, then He is also a God. Jesus never claimed to be God, the Father. He was born into the world as a human being and left as a supreme Spiritual Being. This is the mystery of the creative journey of the earthly phase of the creative journey of the human soul, revealed and demonstrated in Jesus's role of Jesus in controlling the recreation of His own life. This indeed, is the infinite mystery of all mysteries: the mystery of divine power of Jesus Christ in human Creation!

Without me you are nothing.

—Jesus. John 15: 5

Without the Spirit of Christ we are nothing. We need it to be participants in our creation. The mystery of the earthly phase of human creation is this: that at the grand station of death, Jesus was resurrecting and recreating the dead. After resurrection, the revealed created human bore the spirit of Christ (the Spirit of His Father in Him). In Paradise, every resurrected soul, all human souls with eternal life, have the Spirit of Christ, given to us during the earthly phase of our spiritualization by Christ. The mystery of the role of Christ in creation, when revealed in any age, translated into any language, or disclosed under any religious names and symbols, guides human souls to the fuller destiny, to a life with Christ in this world and beyond

In reminiscence, Jesus's everlasting miracle of human creation that revealed His creative power, gave humanity access to the knowledge of Jesus Christ and His Father. The mysteries of Jesus's divine attributes, deemed incomprehensible and inscrutable, were revealed by His epic miracle of human creation. When all the three stages of that Jesus's epic miracle of human creation are completely dissected out on the platform of the absolute power of His Kingdom that manifested, the nature and activities of the Father that sent Him, the mysteries of Jesus's filial relationship with His Father unfolded. We can now answer with confidence, Jesus's question to the apostles: "who do men say that I am?" Jesus insisted on many occasions that He was sent by His Father. "I proceeded forth and came from God; neither came I of myself, but He sent Me." (John 8:42) This resonated in many sayings of Jesus. The fulfillment of Jesus's prediction that He was going to resurrect Himself provided the evidence of the divine origin and authenticity of His words and works. The incomprehensible source of His power became comprehensible. We can now give an answer for Jesus to the persistent question by the Jews: "Who is thy Father and where is He?" It made it easier for us to know His Father and the meaning of Jesus's proclamation, "The Father and I are One." It revealed the most important relationship of human souls with the Father and Jesus Christ. It gave the opportunity to know the intrinsic value of human life. It educated the human soul on how to develop and advance to the highest evolutional level as it strives to be as perfect as the Father in its quest to participate in its own creation. It shines the heavenly light to the invisible staircase where all the evolutional activities of creation are moving. This is the "true Light which lights everyone that comes into the world." (John 1:9) It propelled the fully created human spirits to the divine trinity with the Father and Jesus Christ.

For this end was I born, and for this cause came I unto the world.

—Jesus

If that union with the Father and Jesus Christ is real and the creative powers of Jesus Christ and His Father is true as demonstrated in the epic miracle by Jesus, then there must be a universal vehicle in which this union and creative process can be practically demonstrated and realized by all mankind. There must be a vehicle that the entire mankind could see everyone in it. That common vehicle is Jesus's Kingdom of God. That was what Jesus utilized in the three staged everlasting miracle of human creation. In it lays the secret of human life and the infinite trinity of the human souls with the Spirit of the Father and Jesus Christ. By the proclamation that His Father gave Him all powers and authority on earth and in Heaven, Jesus also enthroned Himself as a Lord and a Creator of human beings. These are what I have been trying to reveal in the entire epistemology of this new Christianity of Christ.

That Christ may dwell in your hearts by faith; that ye, being rooted and grounded in love, May be able to comprehend with all saints what is the breadth, and length, and depth, and height; And to know the love of Christ, which passeth knowledge, that ye might be filled with all the fulness of God.

—Ephesians 3:17-19

Perhaps, a clear vision of the human transcendental transformation to divine status as demonstrated by Jesus Christ could be what we need in order to realize that the world is borderless and belongs to all of us equally. Perhaps, this vital information, rejected by people of Jesus's time, trampled by Christianity as prescribed, proclaimed and practiced today, ignored by religious leaders and powers of this world seeking earthly power and glory, is what we need as to see that we are one humanity with the same destiny. This the life-giving vital knowledge that Jesus died for is what we need to execute what H.I.M. Haile Selassie, in his address to the United Nations in October, 1963, branded as "the noblest aspirations of man: abjuration of force in the settlement of disputes between states; the assurance of human rights and fundamental freedoms for all without distinction as to race, sex, language or religion; the safeguarding of international peace and security." If we understand this mystery of the role of Christ in creation and the *modus operandi* of its execution, it will help us see that killing one another, inter-religious animosity, religious crusades, fragmentation within Christianity as in other religions, racial discrimination, claims of individual, national or religious superiority, survival of the fittest at the expense of the poor, and all other evil activities of the world, are shameful and of no value.

In the light of what I have recovered from the works and words of Christ and revealed in this treatise, we have to rethink and reform our actions. It is my hope that all inhabitants of this world, would finally turn around and accept Jesus's invitation to enter into His Kingdom inherit the eternal life and build on this bondage of infinite love, mercy, compassion, forgiveness, obedience to the will of the Father and the commandments of Christ as catalysts in that fellowship, as we pursue our goal to be fully created as was demonstrated by Jesus's miracle of human creation.

You were a spectator in the timeless auditorium and watched Jesus's timeless miracle of human creation. Today, you are no longer a spectator. You are already in it. It is a model of your own creative journey. Put on your best attire, bring your family, invite all your friends and learn how to prepare to meet your Creators

In Him was life; and the life was the light of men. And the light shines in darkness; and the darkness comprehended it not. That was true Light, which lights everyone that comes into the world.

—John 1:4-5, 9

I am the light of the world.

—Jesus. John 8:12

Believe in the light, that ye may be the children of light.

—John 12:36

CHAPTER 7

WHO ARE WE? WHY ARE WE HERE?

The Kingdom of God is within you.

—Luke 17:21

Human being is a spirit striving to express itself to be fully created. If you have been reading this epiphany, you already know who you are and why you are here. The knowledge of the Kingdom of God reveals what is a human being and the spiritual life and power we are not aware we possess. Jesus told His apostles: "You know not what manner of spirit ye are of." (Luke 9:55)

> *They* (the apostles) *are not of this world, even as I am not of this world.*
>
> *—John 17:16*

> *Ye are from beneath; I am from above; ye are of this world, I am not of this world.*
>
> *—Jesus. John 8:23*

From the above reference, this terrestrial environment is our first home. That we are of this world implies that our earthly existence is the first time we have manifested in physical form. If we are "from beneath and are of this world" then Adam and Eve never lived anywhere but on this planet. They never lived in any Paradise before their earthly life on this planet. They were not created in Paradise and then sent to the planet Earth because they sinned. Many have looked for the garden where Adam and Eve ate the forbidden fruit, and never found it. One may argue that the time they lived on this planet would be considered a Paradise compared with our current earthly life. Adam and Eve were never driven from any Paradise. They underwent the same earthly phase of human creative evolution as we are experiencing now. We have committed sins more horrendous than Adam and Eve's, and yet God has not banished us to another planet. We were told that they ate the forbidden apple. As of today, we still do not know what that apple is. We were told that they disobeyed God. Perhaps, we should know what that disobedience so that we may not fall into the same trap.

We are still not sure of the origin of mankind. However, that origin did not start with Adam and Eve as reported in the Old Testament. At present, the origin of human species is beyond human comprehension. What originated from the Jews are the apocalyptic and eschatological views of the future history of mankind. The Jews popularized them and planted them the Gospel. The Christians adopted it and today they are still looking for the second coming of Christ and the end of the world when Christ would come to judge the living and the dead and the New Jerusalem will descend from heaven. As of now Christ has not appeared in the clouds of heaven with His angels. The glorified Spirit of the risen Christ is still very active in this world.

Let us assume that Adam and Eve were created humans, the most important question is this: who is the God that created them-the God of Moses or God, the Father of Jesus Christ? It was Moses who reported human creation in the book of Genesis and credited it to the God that revealed Himself to Him. What I have been reporting in this treatise-and will continue to do so in the next epiphany-is that Jesus gave us proof that the earthly stages of human creation is controlled by Him and His Father and not the God revealed by Moses. There are many sayings of Jesus Christ that that revealed that He and His Father also control the post resurrection life eternal life. If, as I have presented in this treatise that Jesus and His Father control the evolutionary transcendental transformation of human earthly life, and eternal life as verbalized many times by Christ, it stands to reason that they also control the pre-earthly human life. In essence, the God of Moses is not involved in human creation. This is the deep mystery of Jesus's everlasting miracle of the earthly stages of human creation with the Spirit of His Father in Him. Jesus came into this world as a human being. By using Himself as a model in the epic miracle of human creation, Jesus revealed who we are and why we are here.

Jesus had insisted that the Kingdom of God is within us. In essence, the Spirit of His Father is within us. He was the first to alert mankind of this divine element of a God within us. All the other Gods isolated themselves as being part of us but have this mysterious power to control us. They are outside us rather than within us. They punish us if we disobey their orders and may even take our lands. The merciful loving Father that Jesus revealed to us would not have driven Adam and Eve away from His Paradise; that was originally prepared for them; to this harsh environment we call the planet Earth. All of us, including Adam and Eve, "are from beneath, we are of this world." Many of us know that this is not our final destination. We are yet to be perfected and participate in our earthly stages of our creation. We are being prepared for our final destination, when we will transform into spiritual beings in the image and likeness of the angelic hosts. This divine manifestation of humans is the everlasting life. The Good News is that divine elements of the Kingdom of God shut within us are not bad but good. The experience and manifestation of the divine elements of the Kingdom that is within is the key to this everlasting life. Perhaps we have been looking at the wrong places to find the garden, the original Paradise of the God of Moses. Maybe we have to look within us to find the gateway to the real Paradise of God, the Father of Jesus Christ.

The entrance to the earth is by birth and is common to all humans. The process of conception and development of the human embryo is human metamorphosis: a process that is beyond human comprehension. At what stage the inherited soul enters the developing fetus, we don't know. This is the infinite curiosity in the miracle of pre-earthly life of the newborn.

The wind bloweth were it listeth, you cannot tell where it comes from.

—Jesus

Likewise, we see the newborn: a new soul clothed with the physical body but we do not know where it came from. However, we do know that in this miracle of pre-earthly life that the creative process for the formation of the physical body to cloth the soul of the newborn started in the uterine environment: the first home environment for the alien body. The planet earth is the next environment where the created human beings are temporarily housed before the next phase in the new creation process that Jesus initiated with His Kingdom of God.

The physical body {the bones and flesh} is not standing still awaiting its demise. It is constantly undergoing evolutionary changes adapting to its earthly environment. Most importantly, the physical body has an intrinsic program. It is programmed to undergo staged evolutionary changes that are the same in all human species. This alien body of all mankind and all living animals must pass through stages of childhood, adolescence, middle age, old age, and eventually crumple to dust. This is the fate of the body. But before its demise, it has served its purpose, housing the soul of humankind and perhaps the inactivated invisible spiritual body that is released at the resurrection. Many infants are in the wombs waiting to be born. Many people are in their homes, hospitals, nursing homes and hospice, oblivious of their conditions or environments regardless of their religious, social or national status, waiting to die. This consistency and unabated life cycle in the destiny of mankind refers only to the programmed alien body and not to the human soul and its spiritual body as was showcased on Easter. It is possible that the created spiritual human being-the new creation-moves from one spiritual Kingdom to another until its final evolution to its final stage.

We did not enter this world in sin. Go to any nursery in any hospital, take a good look at the new born babies and tell me if they are all sinners. Nay, they were not born in sin. Look at the children around you, are they sinners? Nay they are not. Jesus said, "Suffer not the little children to come unto me, and forbid them not; for of such is the Kingdom of God" He subsequently put His hand on them and blessed them.

> *"Take heed that ye despise not one of these little ones; for I say unto you, That in heaven their angels do always behold the face of my Father which is in heaven"*

—Matthew 18:10

Our mothers did not conceive us in sin and did not deliver us in sin. This conception of being born in sin is like a dark cloud over the entire humanity and made it impossible for us comprehend the mission of Jesus of Nazareth or understand the spiritual events at Golgotha. Additionally, it formed a smoke screen, preventing us from knowing who we are, why we are here and the destiny of the immortal human spirit. There is no passage in the Gospel that Jesus said we were born in sin. And there was no place in the narratives of the Gospel where Jesus picked up a child and told the child a sinner or a liar and that He has forgiven his or her sin. Jesus called the Jewish forefather's murderers and liars. "Ye are of your father the devil, and the lusts of your father ye will do. He was a murderer from the beginning, and abode not in the truth, because there is no truth in him.........For he is a liar, and the father of it." (John. 8:44) But that did not imply that any Jewish child was born in sin or a liar.

You know not what manner of spirit you are of.

—Luke 9:55

We do now know how creation happens. However, people in Palestine on Easter witnessed the end result of it. What made us who we are began before human conception. People of many religions, scientists, philosophers, and theologians are desperately searching for the origins of human creation. It is an insatiable inscrutable mystery. However, the origin of our being is on this Planet Earth. Probably, it all started from the particles in the water we drink or in the ocean. Jesus said that we are born of water and of Spirit.

Verily, I say unto thee, except a man is born of water and of the Spirit, he cannot enter into the Kingdom of God.

—John 3: 5

From the above reference, the initiation of our being started with what is in the water. This however is beyond the scope of this current epiphany. I have limited my efforts to the staged earthly evolutionary creative process that started from reproductive birth and ends in the spiritual birth of mankind as was demonstrated by Christ. The end result of it was witnessed on Easter. It is still going on. This evolutionary phase will end here when all the created spiritual beings will be gone to other spiritual worlds. How long it will take for them to get to the final destination is unknown as there are many spiritual worlds in the invisible Universe. Some may even accompany Christ to the kingdom of the dead that they too must hear His voice: the words of His Father and have the knowledge of His kingdom of God. If they are willing to enter into it and have the experience of it, they would go with Him to the Father. Human creation is a continuous process, still unfinished. It is irrepressible and will continue, even today and through the end of time, as the Father planned.

Why would God, the Father, and Jesus not leave us alone to do as we please: to love or hate, kill or be killed, sing or cry, then die and be free at last-free from racism and discrimination, free from holy wars, free from dogmas and human doctrines, free from diseases and natural disasters, free from the Devil (although nobody has seen the Devil), free from making our homes in refugee camps and free from the influence from other Gods? The answer is simple: God, the Father and Jesus Christ are still creating and protecting us in ways that we do not understand. The fact that they are still creating us is foreign to many people, even the Christians who still believe in the creation as portrayed by Moses in the book of Genesis.

The human beings we see today are incomplete images of what the Father and Christ are creating. We are human beings with bodies and souls being created to attain full expression as spiritual beings. Jesus's Kingdom of God is involved in this transcendental transformation. Jesus died and resurrected Himself to show us the final image of us: the full created human being. Who are we then that God loves us and takes such an interest in us? What are His expectations and His reason for this earthly life cycle of all humans? Human existence has a purpose and this purpose cannot be changed or modified. It was the same in the past, the same today and will remain the same in the future. Life on this planet earth is not an illusion. It has intrinsic value. It is a journey to God, the Father of Jesus.

We know very little about ourselves. Our knowledge of the universe is rudimentary. The shift from seeing ourselves as inhabitants of the earth whose duty is to live, have children then to die, to seeing ourselves as an expression of what the Father and Jesus Christ are creating, living here as temporary home, is a major shift in understanding who we are and why we are here. In this earthly phase of human creative evolution, the physical body must die: the hunt and the hunted; the evil, and the good, the just and the unjust, the victor and the defeated, the Christians, the Jews, the Muslims, people of other religions, the poor, and the rich, the people that live in big cities and those that live in run-down villages, the trial lawyer who has not lifted a little finger to help a sick patient and the doctor whose duty is to help sick people and has accomplished that duty with compassion and love.

At the end of it all, the complex human flesh and bones turns into ash and blends with the soil making the ground fertile, supporting the plants and indirectly other animals that supported him during the early life cycle. The plants and the animals and all living things are subject to the same fate, Even the earth planet will be subject to the same fate. It too will be void of all living things. Even the mighty oceans will no longer be a habitat for any living thing. It too would have served its purpose in the evolutionary life cycle of its inhabitants. The earth would position itself as a big star in the galaxy, with volcanic eruptions that may mimic supernova eruptions. The entire water in all the streams, rivers and oceans may either be completely frozen or exhibit such a high temperature that nothing survives. It is possible that the sun would be the instrument to be used in this accomplishment of the earth's demise for the fulfillment of all things. It could be ten thousand years, one million or one billion years before the fulfillment and the completion of all the evolutionary process. The time period for this event is one of the great mysteries of God, the Father that Jesus introduced to the world. But as the sun arises from the East to give light and sets in the West, likewise the fulfillment of all earthly events would mark the beginning of glory for all humans and other living things. There would no longer be any reproductive process, no death, and none of the protean religious sects and institutions, no diseases, no cancer, no diabetes, or hypertension, no stab wounds, no gunshot wounds, no poverty, no nuclear weapons or weapons of mass destruction, no refugee camps or prison cells. It would be all laughter and joy with no tears as the created human beings-now angels-move from one spiritual world to another, obeying the will and the commandments of the Father.

The knowledge of Jesus's epic miracle of the stages in human creation is the hermeneutic key to comprehension of whom we are and why we are here. I have also tried to provide windows for people in their own spiritual journey in search for the true meaning of these earthly phases of life cycle. The world community includes diverse groups: Buddhist, Christians, Muslims, Jews, Hindus, Confucians, Taoists, Shinotoists, members of many religions and many non-religious groups. There is no superiority of one group over the other. Who we are, is the common factor that unites human beings of all races, nationalities and religion. It was the common factor in the past. It is the common factor today. It will remain the common factor for the future generations. Any conception of who we are that fails to embrace the entire world community would be grossly inadequate and unacceptable. Despite the protean national, racial, cultural, and religious diversities, there is only one human race under one God. The only thing that is different is the uncontrolled variations in the inheritance and the environmental circumstances amidst which our lives are set. By environmental circumstances, I refer to the period in history: the nationality, the social and religious status into which one's life is set.

We don't pick our parents, nationality or skin colors. In the most part a child born into a Christian family becomes a Christian. A child born into a Muslim family becomes a Muslim. Children born in poor countries did not uproot or destroy God's design and as a punitive measure God directed their being born in those countries. It may seem that God created inferior human beings. But this is not true. Death makes the racial profile, the nationality, the body stature, the religious orientation and the social states irrelevant and of lesser order. The genetic variations have also produced anatomic differences, changes in skin pigmentations, deformity and other abnormalities. This range of variations in the human race has immensely contributed to our confused state on who we are. We have witnessed the creation of test-tube babies, the cloning of sheep (Dolly), the embryonic stem research with the hope of producing transplantable organs and tissues for the alien perishable body. Genome scientists are implanting human genes in animals, creating crossbreeds called chimeras. In animal laboratories, pigs are engineered with human genes that help make their kidneys, hearts and other organs and tissues suitable for transplanting into people. Transgenetic science is a wonderful concept for treatment of diseases. However, if we can learn anything from history of the human species and science, human beings of yesterday, today, and tomorrow will remain essentially the same.

The biologic process by which all humans are created is the same -by birth. The way the earthly life ends is the same-by death. Despite the cultural diversities, the scientific advances, protean religious orientations, the unity and the biologic integrity of the human species has never been broken. The physical body that clothes the inherited soul of man is the same yesterday, today and will remain the same in the future. It will crumple to dust. The basic anatomy and physiology of all humans are the same. The molecular and the genomic functions are the same except for a few environmental alterations. Our brains have more than one hundred billion nerve cells and more than a trillion supporting cells. The function of the brain is mind boggling. Its processing and analytical functions are beyond human understanding. It sends signals to the genes that control all human functions and activities. If we know truly who we are, then we have discovered a higher purpose in life and our collective role in it.

We have no control of our entry into this earth or our exit from it. We have no control over the earth environment we live in. We have no control of its natural forces the hurricanes, volcanoes, seasonal weather variations, earthquakes, plagues, and many other adverse conditions. We have no control of the sunset or sunrise. Without the sun, I doubt if there will be any living thing on earth. History and science have shown that we have indeed destroyed a good part of our planet and are still doing so. From what we know today and judging from the life expectancy of the past generation, everyone on the planet earth will be dead over the next one hundred and forty years. The earth over the same period will be inhabited by new generation. Mankind will not end the use of force to settle disputes, and kill one another, until we understand who we are. Many of Jesus' words on who we are better understood when contemplated against the background of His kingdom of God, His epic miracle of human creation, the nature of the God that He revealed and His role of Jesus and His Father in creation.

Many people have not been able to comprehend who we are and why we are here because of the artificial natural diversity of humankind: the diverse nationality, the ethnicity, the skin color, and racial and religious diversities. Since humanity has advanced to this stage in its physical alien body evolution, we must not only respect and appreciate the human national and religious diversities;

we must protect and defend it, not by killing or territorial conquest but by opening the doors of the inherited spirit of God that is in all humans. The result would be the outpouring of true love, peace, and compassion for our fellow humans, long suffering; gentleness, joy, mercy, compassion, goodness, faith, meekness, temperance, obedience of the will and commandments of God, our Father. On this non-aggressive approach must rest our greatness and evolution of our human spirits for God-human spirit experience and manifestations. If the doors of deception, prejudices, injustice, jealousy, hatred, hypocrisy, greed, and malice were closed, everything earthly would appear as God had intended: finite but immaculate and heavenly.

The future of mankind will have one religion, no Temples, no Cathedrals and no places of worship built with human hands. What they will have is a true living God who is worshiped in spirit and in truth in our hearts. At that time, mankind will be prototypes of that God. They will be perfected as that God they worship.

Be ye therefore perfect as the Father who is in heaven.

—Jesus

Jesus saw that future of mankind and predicted its glorious end if we are willing to be participants. For now there seem to be an impassable barrier to that future. First, mankind worships many Gods. I believe that before it is all over, more Gods will be introduced to mankind. If you worship any God at all, you would like to know who that true living God will be. Second, for any group to proclaim that the God they worship will be that true God they must provide evidence that He is the Creator of mankind. Third, they must provide that the God they worship controls the intrinsic life of the created mankind both here on earth and after death. Fourth, they must reveal verifiable evidence that the same God kept all His promises to mankind. Fifth, the appointed Executioner of His will on Earth must give definitive evidence that He came from that God. Sixth, that appointed Executioner must give us proof of the nature of that God by the epitome of His life examples. Seventh, that Executioner must give us what the Jews identified as "sign from heaven." For Jesus, the search for that God is over. In essence the game played on human consciousness by other Gods is over. The full spectrum of Jesus's everlasting miracle of the earthly stages of human creation was the sigh from heaven.

I want to know God's thoughts.......... the rest are details.

—Albert Einstein.

God's thoughts for humans are simple: He wants us to inherit Jesus's Kingdom of God and through what was accomplished at Golgotha and beyond, return to Him as perfected spirits, bearing within us, all the attributes of Jesus's Kingdom of God: love, compassion, righteousness, charity, forgiveness, justice, and mercy in victory. The perfected spirit must be willing to obey the will of God as the angels do in heaven. This spiritual evolutional development and participation in the earthly stages of the miracle of human creation with the power of Jesus's Kingdom of God as to be fully created as perfected spiritual beings is the only reason why we are here. That was what the Father planned and what is in His will. Jesus had insisted the Kingdom of God is within us and that we are unaware of the power of that Kingdom of God that is within us. Jesus was sent down by His Father as a human being. He allowed Himself to be humiliated, condemned to death, crucified and died as to reveal that vital information to mankind and demonstrate the creative power of that Kingdom of God. He used Himself as a model. In doing so, Jesus revealed His role in human creation.

Our task is to enter into Christ's Kingdom of God, experience it and seek and learn how to manifest that experience in preparation for our journey to the Father, our God. It has been said that money is the root of all evils, but it is not so. The root of all evils is ignorance of Jesus's Kingdom of God, who we are, why we are here and our final destiny. This is the era of biological, chemical, nuclear weaponry, global terrorism, global warming, aids epidemic, massive environmental pollution with emergence of protean deadly diseases, cancer, tribal and national wars. The world is at the brink of self-destruction. Mankind despite its scientific and technical advances has again earned the highest mark in inhumane treatment of its fellow beings. One of the great tragedies in human history is the profound conflicts in places where Buddha, Moses, Jesus of Nazareth and Prophet Mohammad gave directions for human spiritual growth. It is also perpetuated by groups and nations who claim they abide by the divine laws and orders but fail to do so by the examples if their lifestyles. The concept of inferior race, superior race, superior religion, inferior religion, poor nations, super nations, developed nations and underdeveloped nations is a portrayal of ignorance of who the Father is, what His will is, how He works, and His design for all humanity. It is the greatest betrayal of the trust and love Jesus bestowed on us. Many nations and individuals have used this ignorance and mistrust to exploit what divides us for their shameless selfish gains.

The time has come and now is when all human communities must be taught in the basic understanding of who we are, why we are here and our common destiny. The future of mankind, the continuation of the process of creation by God, the preservation of the planet earth depends on it. If Christianity is to "lounge deep for a draw" then Christianity must reveal to the world the tools that were made manifest at Golgotha for activation, promulgation, and manifestation of human spirit as it seeks full expression of itself to be fully created.

If one takes a look at the history of humanity, we don't have to be rocket scientists to realize that we are the deadliest enemy of our own kind and the earth's environment. Humanity got on the wrong footing right from the very beginning. One day we would recognize the common humanity and realize that we are all of one kind, that the planet earth is comparable to a uterine environment; that we cannot make any more significant improvement in our civilization, without developing our spirituality simultaneously. The first earthly exposure of all humans is the mother's womb. The second stage is the earth environment. If one contaminates the amniotic fluid, it will adversely affect the fetus. If one contaminates the earth, it will affect all living things and we are seeing the result of such contamination today. The uterine environment and the planet earth can be considered as cocoons or platforms for the accomplishment of God's plan. As the caterpillar by the process of metamorphosis turn into a butterfly, likewise all humans by the process of death and resurrection have to complete the earthly phase of creation as was demonstrated by Jesus in His everlasting miracle of human creation as to be fully created and enter into eternal life. The game is over. You are absolutely in control how it would end for you. Good luck!

I came to give you life and give it to you abundantly.

—Jesus

CHAPTER 8

JEWISH CONCEPT OF SALVATION AND ETERNAL LIFE

"Salvation is of the Jews"

—Jesus. John 4:22

The concept of salvation in the Christian literatures originated from the Jews. It is important that we must first know what is salvation and then examine where it is linked with Jesus's Kingdom of God and eternal life as proclaimed and demonstrated by Christ. The Jews believed that their God made them as a chosen people for Himself. This God delivered them from the Egyptian bondage and promised everlasting fellowship if they keep His laws and commandments. (Exodus 19) They learned from the history of Adam and Eve what that God would do if they disobey Him. The God revealed to them by Moses punished them if they sin against Him by allowing other nations to conquer them. The Jews resorted to repentance and sacrifices for atonement of their sins if they worshipped other Gods or turn away from Him as to maintain that fellowship with Him. They responded with organized festivals: the Feast of Passover, when they sacrificed a lamb without blemish in the Temple for personal redemption and in remembrance for their delivery from the Egyptian bondage; the Feast of Atonement when they sacrificed a goat for cleansing of their nation Israel from their sins. (Leviticus 16:5-11) The initial idea of the Jewish concept of salvation was born: deliverance from their sins and from their enemies and realization of lasting peace and Fellowship with their God. Without sin the concept of salvation will evaporate.

The promise of salvation and glory for Israel came directly from God. (Exodus 14:13, 15:2, Isaiah 45:16–17) The promise of a Savior for this salvation by their God was also conditioned on many other moral and the religious practices of the Jewish people. (Isaiah 45: 21-25) The fellowship with their God and everlasting peace would continue in the Promised Land in Canaan, However, whenever they disobey that God, He punishes them for their sins by allowing other nations to defeat them, with many being carried into captivity. Nobody jokes with that God. At a stage in the history of the Jewish people, ten tribes out of twelve, just vanished, probably carried into captivity or killed. Probably, it was the Assyrian King Sennacherib during the reign of Hezekiah that conquered and carried away the ten tribes of Israel.

The followings are needed for the Jewish salvation

The belief that their God will forgive them if they repent of their sins
The belief that the God of Israel will send a Savior, later referred as the Messiah
Strict observing the Sabbath day custom
Remission of guilt (Isaiah 33:24)
Belief in the God Abraham, Isaac and Jacob
Belief in all the covenants of the Jewish people with that God
Practice circumcision
Obedience of the Ten Commandments'

Strict obedience to the laws in Torah and Mishna
Other moral renovations (Jeremiah 31:33)

Subsequently, after the Babylonian captivity, the Jews modified this concept of salvation and introduced an intermediary, a spiritual servant of the Lord, whom God would use to deliver them from their enemies. Although there were no passages in the Old Testament literature that referred to the Messiah or the Anointed One, later by the time of Christ Judaism had evolved to view all the prophetic oracles leading to God's appointed intermediary as the Messiah, the God's Anointed One who would bring salvation to Israel. At that time, "the glory of the Lord shall be revealed, and all flesh shall see it together: for the mouth of the Lord hath spoken." (Isaiah 40:5) The philology of the Messiah pointed to the liberation of the Jews from bondage and to the future role of Israel as the ruler of the spiritual kingdom that God would establish on earth. When Jesus came, the Jews were waiting for the promised Messiah who would free them from the Roman bondage, unite them, restore the glory to Israel, and establish God's kingdom on earth with Jerusalem as the capital. Satan, the Tempter, made use of this Messianic expectation of the Jewish people when he tempted Jesus in the wilderness. (Luke 4:5–7) Jesus did not come to establish any earthly kingdom. Satan was making sure that Jesus would not succumb to the widely held expectation that He was the expected Jewish Messiah. To have succumbed to that satanic temptation would mean that He came as the Jewish Messiah, seeking control of the earthly kingdom.

The Messianic hope was at its peak when Jesus came. When Mary and Joseph took Jesus as a child to the temple, Anna, a prophet, looked at the child Jesus as He who would bring redemption in Jerusalem. The just and devout man, Simon, looked at Jesus as He that would bring glory to Israel. (Luke 2:25-38) After the death of Jesus, Cleopas and his companion had hoped Jesus would bring salvation to Israel. Even the apostles, just before the ascension of their Master, had asked Him; "Will you at this time restore the kingdom to Israel?" The expected Jewish Messiah would bring salvation to the Jews. He would live forever, protecting Israel to the end of time, when He would establish the spiritual kingdom on earth. Jesus did not attempt to demonstrate or assure the Jewish people that He was the one to fulfill their expectation of their conceived idea about salvation. Today the Jews are still waiting for their Messiah. Salvation as conceived by the Jews has nothing to do with Jesus's Kingdom of God. However, with this background information, one can look at salvation as handed down to us as Christians, with the lens of Jesus's Kingdom of God and His words on eternal life.

CHAPTER 9

SALVATION, ETERNAL LIFE AND JESUS'S KINGDOM OF GOD

What does salvation in Jesus as presented to the Christians mean today? What is the connection between salvation as conceived in its present form, and the Kingdom of God and eternal life as proclaimed and demonstrated by Christ? Will its doctrine be applicable to people of other religions today and in future? These are the questions that the Church and Christian theologians must find the answer in today's world, in the scheme of what they handed down to us as salvation. Any doctrine proclaimed by Christ was followed by examples of His lifestyle and demonstrations of the power of His Kingdom of God in miracles to support that doctrine. Jesus's epic miracle of the earthly stages of human creation was such miracle that substantiated His words on the Kingdom of God and eternal life. Was there anything in the lifestyle of Christ before His death that suggested salvation in Him? The answer is no. Was there anything in any of His demonstrations that revealed the meaning of salvation and why we needed it? Many Christians and their leaders pointed to His death. This association of the death of Jesus Christ with salvation is the greatest obstacle to Jesus's everlasting miracle of the earthly stages of human creation. For the last two thousand years, it made it impossible to envision and comprehend that miracle. It redirected the Christians to the original sin of Adam and Eve that we all inherited. Their reason is simple. Without sin, the word salvation will evaporate from the memory of mankind and water baptism for remission of sins will be eliminated from the sacraments. Then the conspirators that linked the death of Christ with salvation did the impossible by directing us to the Old Testament texts in the book of Isaiah, the prophet of the Jewish salvation, to find the link.

Since the death and resurrection of Christ, can the Christians affirm that they have experienced salvation in Jesus? If so, how did they experience it? If the words and the deeds of Christ points to salvation, if Christ brought salvation and if, as proclaimed, salvation is only through Christ, then all Christians must turn to Christ to find the meaning of salvation. If however, the reason why His Father sent Him to the world had nothing to do with salvation of mankind as prescribed and proclaimed by Christians, then the Christian conception of salvation would be considered as one of the greatest obstacle to the Christianity of Christ and a hindrance to the comprehension of the earthly phase of the creative evolution of the human soul to its glorious end. On the other hand, if a deeper reflections of salvation, when reviewed without the Jewish lens was an offer of that definite gift of His Father through Jesus to human souls, then salvation, when articulated with the works and words of Jesus Christ becomes an indispensible tool in the comprehension of the creative evolution of the human soul to its glorious end. Outside the Jewish players, and the Jewish mindsets of salvation of the apostles and Paul, what the Christians proclaimed as salvation pointed only in one direction: the invisible staircase of the Jewish God revealed by Moses and to many of the apocalyptic utterances of the Jewish prophets.

The meaning of salvation is not the same for the members of Judaism and Christians, as they are rooted in two different parallel trajectories. How did Christ define salvation? Can we put all together to find what it means to us and our current human life? If we are to penetrate into the Christian concept of salvation, we must look at Peter's proclamations on salvation, the changes the apostles, Paul, and the early Christians adopted at first Apostolic Council in Jerusalem in the year A.D 47. We must find out what that meeting was all about. We must find out how Paul proclaimed salvation to the Greco-Roman converts and his doctrine of sin. The apostles and many of the early Christians were all Jews, and many of their views were heavily Hebrew in nature. They remained liberal Pharisees to the very end of their lives. They obeyed the laws in Torah and the ceremonial laws. The Jews did not believe that Jesus is the expected Messiah. Likewise the apostles and Paul did not call Jesus the Messiah. Peter simply identified Him as the Christ, the Son of the living God. Jesus did nothing to suggest He is the Messiah.

My suggestion to all who engage in the philology of Christian concept of salvation is to first study the Old Testament literature. They have to pay attention to the God revealed by Moses, the utterances of the Prophets, the Jewish concept of salvation and the religious and ritual laws connected with that salvation. The next thing to do is to read the four Gospel records, paying particular attention to apocalyptic Kingdom of God incorporated in those records as the sayings of Jesus. The meaning of the salvation as proclaimed by Peter and Paul, when viewed without the Jewish lens, the role of Christ in creation and the nature of the God, the Father of Jesus, the definition of human life, all point to the trajectory of Jesus's Kingdom of God and its goal.

What Christ presented to us in the Gospel is a loving merciful God who will not harm His enemies or any of His human creation. The God of Moses presented in the Old Testament texts drove out Adam and Eve from the Paradise because of sin and punishes the Jews any time they sin or transgress His laws. Forgiveness, love, compassion and mercy are the hallmarks of our association with Jesus and the Father presented to us. The bedrock of that association is rooted in Jesus's Kingdom of God ant the eternal life linked with that Kingdom. The salvation by the God of Moses to the Jewish people-the chosen people-is conditioned on strict observances of the laws that He gave to Moses and on the ceremonial laws. Did the Father of Jesus send Him down from heaven to sacrifice Himself on the cross to quell the anger of the Jewish God or His own anger? There was no report from Jesus that His Father is angry with mankind. We are dealing with two Gods: the God of Moses and the Father, the God of Jesus Christ. Later on in history, Prophet Mohammed introduced another God that he called Allah. There may even be more Gods out there. At this level of our evolutional emancipation, we just do not know. We need time to sort it out. We need our spirituality to evolve and develop more. What I have presented on God, the Father of Jesus is what I recovered from the Gospel. I believe in that Father and in Jesus Christ. We can go on dancing to the music of salvation as handed down to us by the Christian leaders and theologians and go on doing what we know best: accumulating earthly treasures at expense of others and killing one another. We can leave Judaism and the Old Testament alone and search the Gospel of Christ for the revelations of all the mysteries of His words and works as proclaimed and demonstrated by Him. Our glorious future depends on the vital knowledge of Jesus's words and works. Our glorious future has nothing to do with salvation. There are no preconditions demanded of us by God, our Father in heaven as to enter into Jesus's Kingdom of God and inherit eternal life. Salvation as conceived by the Jews and the Christians has no link with Jesus's Kingdom of God or eternal life as proclaimed prescribed and demonstrated by Christ.

The reason why I am writing this book is to make the understanding of Christianity of Christ easy. The words of Jesus Christ are not word of salvation but words of eternal life. Peter said to Jesus: "Lord, to whom shall we go? Thou hast the word of eternal life." (John 6:68) The Gospel of "The Gospel is the power of God to salvation." (Romans 1:6) The concept of salvation pointed only the Jewish God and the history of Israel in sin, punishment by that God, repentance and forgiveness by the same God. Israel depended on salvation for their apocalyptic future. The Gospel of Christ is not the power of God to salvation. If that God is the Father of Christ then, the Gospel of Christ is the Gospel of His Kingdom of God. It revealed His Father as the only true God, Himself, how we can enter into that kingdom, inherit eternal life and be partakers in the nature of His Father and participants in our own creation.

The various interpretations of salvation are readily available in the doctrines of Judaism and Christianity and in many passages of both the Old and the New Testament scriptures. Any interpretation of what is salvation, how to receive it, how it manifests on the individual who received it and its intrinsic value to the human soul, must look at the Gospel of Christ and the Kingdom of God that came. To understand salvation we must know the meaning of Jesus's kingdom of God and why He died. Jesus died and resurrected Himself to reveal the prototype of what He and His Father were creating. There is no transcendental gulf between His death and resurrection. There is a transcendental synthesis, a direct connection, between Jesus's death and His resurrection. All Christian's proclamations on salvation-the doctrine of sin, atonement, the conquest of death, the defeat of Satan, the sufferings and the death of Christ, justification, faith, grace, and sacraments-and what it means to mankind today, must be viewed with the lens of Jesus' Kingdom of God-His Spirit in human souls, His death and resurrection, is a the platform Jesus used to display to the world what His Father and Himself are creating: the spiritual mankind, who will ultimately seek for the blessings, the righteousness and fellowship with God, the Father and Jesus Christ. All other venues are closed. In essence, all venues for exploration of Salvation for the Christians are closed. Salvation is for the Jews.

The hallmarks of Jesus' saving activities and the gift of eternal life are:

Mercy and compassion
Love that extends to the enemy
Forgiveness of sins-not by His death
Healing of the sick
Willingness to pardon those who transgress against Him and His Father,
Delivery of the gift from His Father-the Spirit of His Father-to mankind,
Instruction to mankind on how to enter into His Kingdom of God, experience it and participate in the earthly stages of their own creation

The metaphysical drama at Golgotha did not bring salvation as perceived by the Jews and many Christians. What was finished at Golgotha did not wipe away the sins of the world or quell the anger of the loving merciful Father that Jesus revealed to us. The spiritual event at Golgotha was a stage in Jesus's epic miracle of human creation that was powered by His Kingdom of God. It directed mankind to participate in the earthly phase of creation, seek fellowship and divine union with Him and His Father.

For God sent not His Son into the world to condemn the world; but that the world through Him might be saved.

—Jesus. John 3:17

The saving activities of Jesus Christ as demonstrated in His words and works have nothing to do with salvation as perceived by today's

Christians and the Jews. Jesus's saving activities are rooted in the power of His Kingdom of God and in His epic miracle of human creation. Jesus did not label them as salvation. Jesus used the word 'salvation' only once in His teaching and relegated that concept to the Jews.

Salvation is of the Jews.

—Jesus

Jesus never said: 'I am the Salvation' The encounter of Jesus Christ with the rich man Zaccheus is the best introduction on how the Jews in that one instance, tried to convince us that Jesus embraced the Jewish concept of salvation. (Luke 19:1–10 Jesus's core message was the Kingdom of God and eternal life. Jesus had identified Himself as one who is authorized to give that Spirit of the Father in Him-the Spirit of Christ-to human souls. The apostles and many others had received that Spirit. It is possible that all that Jesus said to Zaccheus when He entered his house is this: 'the Kingdom of God-my Spirit; has come to you and your house hold.' That would be in consistent with what Jesus had been doing in cities and villages, giving His Spirit to people who believe in Him. Jesus Christ grossly changed the concept of salvation started by the Jews, introduced new concepts of eternal life through the power of His Kingdom of God. Temple services are essential component in the Jewish concept of salvation. However, Jesus said to the Samaritan woman, "Woman, believe me, the hour cometh, when ye shall neither in this mountain (the Samaritan temple on Mount Gerizim), nor yet at Jerusalem (the Jewish temple) worship the Father. Ye worship ye know not what; we know what we worship; for salvation is of the Jews. But the hour cometh and now is, when the true worshippers shall worship the Father in spirit and in truth; for the Father seeketh such to worship Him." (John 4:21–23) Here again, when the subject of salvation surfaced, Jesus quickly revealed and enthroned His Father as the Spirit we must worship in spirit and in truth.

In reminiscence, Jesus Christ did not preach salvation. He is well versed in the Jewish concept of salvation and said that "salvation is of the Jews" and made no further comment on it.

*Learn of me........*Jesus

CHAPTER 10

THE MYSTERY OF PAUL'S MAKEOVER SALVATION, ETERNAL LIFE AND THE KINGDOM OF GOD

The mystery of Paul's concept of salvation, when revealed as I will show in this Epiphany, points also to Jesus's kingdom of God. When Paul's doctrine on salvation is completely dissected, and when all the Jewish components are completely routed out from it, what is left is Jesus's kingdom of God in action and salvation of Israel that is rooted in sin and punishment of Israel in particular and the whole world in general.

> *My speech and preaching was not with enticing words of man's wisdom, but in demonstration of the Spirit and of the power, that your faith should not stand in the wisdom of men, but in the power of God.*

> —Paul. 1 Corinthians 2:4-5

In essence, Paul, having received Jesus's kingdom of God in him (Christ in me) manifested it by demonstrating the power of it, proclaimed and inaugurated it in the Greco-Roman Empire and in

Asia Minor as salvation. What then is the meaning of salvation and the Kingdom of God to Paul?

Christ did not send me to baptize, but to proclaim the Gospel.

—1Corinthians 1:17

For I am not ashamed of the gospel of Christ: for it is the power of God unto salvation to everyone that believeth; to the Jew first, and also to the Greek.

—Romans 1:16

What Gospel did Paul really preach? Is it the Gospel of the kingdom of God or the Gospel of salvation? The Gospel that Jesus proclaimed featured prominently on His Kingdom of God. If one can accurately define the Father's task for Jesus, why He sent Jesus to the world, then the whole Gospel of Christ, proclaimed and demonstrated by Christ, would reveal all its secrets. The password to the secrets is Jesus's Kingdom of God. The way to Christ and to understanding what Paul said and accomplished should be made easy to everyone. The messages of words and works of Christ by the apostles and Paul to the Greco-Roman Empire or to any world community, must be viewed with the lens of Jesus's Kingdom of God. To understand Paul's concept of salvation we must look at the following:

Paul as a Jew, the Hebrew of the Hebrews
His knowledge of Jesus' Kingdom of God, His death and resurrection
Paul's life experience, his works and his belief in the risen Christ.
Prevailing Greco-Roman religious and imperial theology when their emperors are considered as Gods.

His reformed religious objectives and visions.
His zeal to recruit people for Christ that they may "walk in" a manner worthy of God who calls you unto His own kingdom and glory." (Thessalonians. 2:12)
His ambition to recruit co-workers for Jesus' kingdom of God (Colossians 4:11)

Paul had a clear vision of his task assigned to him by Christ. Paul proclaimed what he called salvation but it is deeply rooted in the Spirit of Christ in him-Jesus's Kingdom of God in action within his soul

Salvation which is in Jesus Christ for the eternal glory of mankind.

— II Timothy 2:10

Salvation that leads to righteousness of the human souls for all who believe in Christ.

—Romans 10:9-13

Salvation is not in Christ. What is in Christ is His Kingdom of God (the Spirit of His Father). Jesus was given the authority to bestow it to human souls for eternal life as we seek for the fulfillment of our glorious destiny. Salvation does not lead to the righteousness of the human souls for all who believe in Christ. Jesus's Kingdom of God within human souls leads to righteousness for all who believe in Christ. Jesus instructed us to: "Seek after the Kingdom of God and its righteousness and everything will be added unto us." The Spirit of the risen Christ in human souls is the key component of Pauline salvation theology. But the truth is that the same Spirit of Christ is the key component in Jesus's Kingdom of God.

The mystery of what happened to Paul on his way to Damascus was like the wind from heaven that blew on him. When it was all over, Paul found Christ in him. Have you ever wondered why

Christ chose Paul, despite the fact that he was, at that time persecuting the Christians? What did Jesus find in Paul as to make him 'a chosen vessel'? (Acts 9:15-16) Jesus did not choose Paul to stop the persecution of the Christians. The persecution of the Christians persisted for a long time and is still going on today. Paul was also persecuted and finally beheaded in Rome. Peter and the other apostles were men "who are not of this world." (Luke 17:18) Perhaps Paul too, was not from this world. What Paul accomplished for Christianity is yet to be duplicated by anyone. The real question is this: did Jesus choose Paul to spread the message of salvation or that of His Kingdom of God? The Kingdom of God was Jesus's core message during His mission. He demonstrated the power of it and utilized all the divine elements in that Kingdom to successfully accomplish all His works. He continued to lecture the apostles on the Kingdom of God after His resurrection. The concept of salvation had no place in the words and works of Christ. Jesus recruited Paul to reveal what is the Kingdom of God and why they need it to the Greco-Roman people.

After two visits to Jerusalem, Paul left and never came back. He marched to the Greco-Roman Empire with no sword, no armor, no extra sandals, and one coat. He had with him the scripts with which to write. Today we are the benefactors of these records. Paul was guided by:

The voice of the spirit of the risen Christ and his heavenly vision (Acts 9:8).
His own life experience before and after his conversion
His knowledge of the God that Moses revealed to Israel
His knowledge of the Jewish religion (he was tutored under Gamaliel)
His knowledge of Greek politico-religious theologies (He was born as a Roman in Tarsus a city in the Roman of Empire)

His knowledge of Jesus Kingdom of God (he preached the Kingdom of God for three months in Jerusalem before he left)

The voice of Christ that spoke to him again (II Corinthians 12:9)

His knowledge of the mysteries of Christ (Ephesians 3:3-7)

The joy that His sins and transgressions were forgiven

His love for Christ and his Father and the people of the Greco-Roman Empire

His unquenchable resolution to bring that 'Christ' in him to all the Greco-Roman people that Christ may dwell in them for their own glory and fellowship with God, the Father of Jesus Christ to reveal Christ and His Father

As a Hebrew of the Hebrews from the tribe of Benjamin, well-versed in the Hebrew religion, Judaism, and in the Old Testament texts, he knew everything about the salvation of Israel and its people. The Kingdom of God that Jesus proclaimed was new to everybody. Paul did not proclaim Jesus to be the Messiah. However, as a Jew Paul believed in the Jewish Messiah and the promised salvation that would manifest along with it the glory of Israel. As the seed that Christ planted in Paul started to grow, Paul began to see things differently. "We know in part, and we prophesy in part." (Paul, I Corinthians 13: 8-12)

Paul left imprints in all his epistles that, when put together, revealed his concept of the Kingdom of God as it evolved. He was like a general contractor, building a house without a certified architectural design plan. Paul, by his actions, claimed that his design, revealed to him by Christ, was in his head. At the end of it all, a closer observation of what Paul developed and labeled as salvation was consistent with the words and works of Jesus Christ and the Father's plan for mankind. What Paul proclaimed as salvation to the people-Jews and Gentiles and demonstrated by his earthly lifestyle and miracles to them was consistent with what Jesus proclaimed as the Kingdom of God in action. Paul used himself as an example.

What Paul did to the salvation of Israel and its people was in stages. At the first stage, the Apostolic Council in Jerusalem, about 50-51 AD, under the insistence of Paul, decided that the Gentile converts to Christianity were not obligated to keep some of the ceremonial laws like circumcision. However, they were still to be under the conditions prescribed in the Torah for salvation (Acts 15). In the second stage, at the end of his first missionary journal, Paul returned to Jerusalem again, about fourteen years later. It was in response to a revelation, (Gal 2:1-9) to reveal to Peter and other members of the Council, the type of the Gospel, what he was preaching to the Gentiles. (Gal 2:14-21). Paul was already at that time, preaching salvation without referring to the Torah. It was a marked shift from the preconditions set forth by Moses for salvation of Israel and its people. In offering this law-free salvation to the Gentile converts, Paul removed Moses as the mediator and placed Christ as the mediator of salvation. Then Paul did the impossible: Paul removed the nation of Israel in the equation and made salvation a personal affair of humans with the risen Christ. But Paul was not finished. For what he did next, the Jews pursued him from one city to another to kill him. My dear readers you have the right to ask me now what did Paul do next? Be patient.

The Jews had accused Paul of being a pestilent fellow and a mover of sedition among all the Jews throughout the world and a ring leader of the sect of the Nazarenes. (Act 24:5-6). The Jews knew they were not telling the truth about why they were trying to kill Paul. Again, when King Agrippa told Paul he was permitted to speak for himself, Paul said he was being persecuted because he believed in the resurrection of Christ. Paul knew he was not telling the truth. The Pharisees who were persecuting Paul also believed in resurrection as Paul correctly affirmed in his defense. Both parties knew that resurrection was not the issue. What Paul did, like his Master Jesus Christ, was considered a blasphemy. As Paul saw thing more clearly on what Jesus proclaimed, prescribed and demonstrated and with the knowledge of his revelations, Paul like His Master broke the first commandment of Moses and encouraged the Jews and the people in the Greco-Roman Empire to do the same. Paul replaced the God of Moses with the God, the Father of Jesus. Paul called himself, in many texts of his epistles to-the Corinthians, Ephesians, Philippians, Colossians, and Thessalonians-the servant of God, our Father and the Lord Jesus Christ. That was the lethal weapon that lead to his death. After Paul was released from prison, he was finally beheaded by the Jews to silence him.

Paul took the salvation of Israel and its people, cloned it to Jesus' Kingdom of God, enthroned His Father as the true God, and presented it to the Christians, Jews, and the Gentiles in the Greco-Roman Empire as the core element in the Christian faith. When the cloned Pauline salvation is viewed with the Jewish lens, the promised Jewish Messiah, the anticipated glory of Israel, the New Jerusalem, all the prescribed conditions the Jews must fulfill if they sin or transgress the law as to obtain salvation, Moses as the mediator, and the God that spoke to him, simply evaporated. This is the mystery of Paul's concept of salvation. The cloned Pauline salvation started with the risen Christ. Its future is linked with the risen Christ and His Kingdom of God in action. In its transcendent evolution, it is connected with the human soul before and after resurrection as it journeys to its ultimate end as revealed in the Pauline eschatology of the future salvation that is consistent with eternal life. Pauline cloned salvation is centered on the risen Christ and on His Kingdom of God. After two years of imprisonment in Rome, before he was murdered, Paul continued proclaiming Jesus's Kingdom of God and God, as the Father of Jesus Christ. (Romans 14:17; 1 Corinthians 4:20; 6:9-10; 15:24, 50; Galatians 5:21; Ephesians 5:5; Colossians 1:13; 1 Thessalonians 2:2; 2 Thessalonians 1:5, 2 Timothy 4:1, 18)

The story of Pauline cloned salvation is, in effect, the story of the creative evolutionary process of his soul as it journeyed to righteousness, peace, and divine trinity with God, the Father, and the risen Christ. He did not see death in his creative trajectory on the ground that Jesus had died for him. For Paul, resurrection was not on the creative trajectory pathway for him to achieve his glory. For him he was already resurrected. Paul was looking forward to the time when he and others, dead or alive, would ascend to meet the risen Christ in the clouds of heaven.

The spirit of the risen Christ came to him because Jesus died and resurrected. Without the resurrection, it became impossible for Paul to preach Jesus's kingdom of God. Paul manifested the power of that Kingdom with the Christ in him, by performing miracles. He lived his life as one who had entered into that Kingdom, inherited the eternal life component of it and manifested his experience of it as partaker of the nature of the Father in that Kingdom. He prepared the human souls in the Greco-Roman Empire as the fertile ground for the implantation of the 'seed' from Christ. Although Paul did not define the meaning of Jesus's Kingdom of God, his writings, His life, his words, and his works represented the meaning of the Kingdom of God and many of its mysteries. Paul, like the apostles, suffered. But to him it was necessary to suffer for the glorious end that awaits mankind. He worked toward "the mark for the prize of the high calling of God in Jesus Christ." (Philippians 3:14) For Paul this high prize is his resurrection.

If by any means I might attain unto the resurrection of the dead. Not as though I had already attained, either were already perfect: but I follow after, if that I may apprehend that for which also I am apprehended of Christ Jesus.

—Philippians 3: 11-12

Paul frequently visited Saints and unknown spirits in the third heaven, heard things not lawful to utter. (2 Corinthians 12: 4) The Spirit of Christ came to him because Jesus died and resurrected. Without the resurrection of Christ, Paul would not have been saved. Paul's proclamation that "without resurrection of Christ, there is no salvation" was a personal experience. Paul did not see himself as a mortal man, but as a divine servant appointed not by any mortal, but by Christ Himself to serve Him and His Father with unquestioned obedience. He lived in Christ and Christ lived in him. Paul, who was already dead in sin before his experience with Christ on his way to Damascus, without any faith in Christ before that encounter, considered himself dead and resurrected in Christ. And will ascend at any time on the day of the Lord.

Paul passed through the stages of what Jesus demonstrated in His epic miracle of human creation. Pauline concept of the cloned salvation was original its conception. He experienced it and manifested its power and divine attributes. It manifested itself as Jesus's Kingdom of God that came. It was rooted in this "Christ in him"-a gift from Christ to his troubled soul. It was the foundation for all his words and works in the Greco-Roman Empire and Asia Minor. It propelled him and all who were willing to come along with him to the infinite trinity of their souls with the Spirit of the risen Christ and His Father. Jesus had said that "I came to give you life and give it to you abundantly." For Paul this life is the Spirit of the risen Christ in him. "It is not I that live, but Christ that lives in me." "If any man be in Christ, he is a new man." The core element of Pauline salvation and everything that he preached was the Spirit of the risen Christ in human souls. In doing so, Paul was directing human souls to the trajectory of the earthly phase of human creation in the Greco-Roman Empire and Asia Minor.

But if the Spirit of him that raised up Jesus from the dead dwell in you, he that raised up Christ from the dead shall also quicken your mortal bodies by his Spirit that dwelleth in you.

—Paul Romans 8: 11

Paul embraced Jesus's kingdom of God, not only proclaimed it and exemplified the realization of it, but pushed it to a fathomless spiritual realm, beyond the comprehension of not only his contemporaries but also of today's Christian theologians and authorities. Paul spoke with authority, confidence and wisdom. A guided insight into the mind of that highly educated man-who read many books more than the religious leaders of his time-on what he did, why he did what he had to do, what he fought for without violence or hatred in his heart against those persecuting him, always on the run, revealed a man who in the last years of his life, when he was released from prison, before he was beheaded, "Boldly and without hindrance preached the Kingdom of God and taught about the Lord Jesus Christ." (Acts 28: 31)

CHAPTER 11

PAUL'S DOCTRINE OF SIN ON SALVATION AND ETERNAL LIFE

Now if any man has not the Spirit of Christ,
hr is none of His.

—Paul. Romans 8:9

Paul was Jesus's appointed shepherd to the gentiles in the Greco-Roman Empire. For him, to be saved by Jesus is to be saved by the spirit of the risen Christ in Him. Paul gathered the sheep in the Greco-Roman Empire and in Asia Minor in one fold and gave them practical demonstrations on how to enter into the Kingdom of God. By his works, God, the Father of Jesus was enthroned as the only true God. The Spirit of the risen Jesus Christ was glorified and His kingdom of God illuminated. Without knowing it, Paul built on the one foundation laid by Christ Himself: His Kingdom of God. Paul's life with Christ in him was a manifestation of Jesus's Kingdom of God in action. His works brought the people of the Greco-Roman Empire-dead or alive-to Christ. The big question is this: how did he do it? How did he succeed among people who never heard of Jesus's words or works? Many of them never even heard of Nazareth, or the word salvation. The Romans had crucified many Jews. Jesus was among them and that was the end of the story for them. How did Paul succeed where Emperors-Julius Caesar and Augustus were considered deities-the Sons of God? How did Paul succeed in an Empire with so many Gods that had influenced the minds of the Roman people and built many Temples of worship for them? The architectural designs of those Temples are still unmatched even as of today. Many of the stars of the Universe are still named after those Gods that the Romans worshiped. How did Paul succeed among those people whose ambitions were to plunder, kill, conquer, expand the boundaries of their Empire and carry off their treasures and the people as slaves?

While Peter and other apostles were proclaiming the news of Jesus's resurrection in Jerusalem, Paul took off to the Greco-Roman Empire. To proclaim the news of Jesus's death and resurrection was not enough for conversation among the Gentiles. The tools that Jesus used to get a foothold in Palestine-miracles, parables, sermons- would not work in a place filled with philosophers, sorcerers and idol worshippers. Paul knew that Jesus did not send him to the Gentiles to baptize as Jesus Himself did not baptize.

Christ did not send me to baptize, but to proclaim the Gospel.

—Paul, 1 Corinthians 1:17

Paul tried it anyway. Those he baptized started speaking in tongue language that no one could understand. So he gave it up. That prompted Paul to warn about speaking or praying in tongues. (1 Corinthians 14:13-19) He tried miracles. Paul performed about seven miracles. That was not his strength, so he gave it up.

What then did Paul use to bring the people to Christ? What methods did Paul use to get the hearts ready for the planting of the seeds, the Spirit of Christ, in the souls of the Greco-Roman people? He was not going to tell them about the expected Jewish Messiah. They never heard of any Messiah. So Paul refrained from using the word Messiah. Paul preached a salvation that had nothing to do with salvation of the Jews. If you were Paul and found yourself in that situation, what methods would you use to get your message about Christ and His plan for mankind to the people? How would you reveal God, the Father of Jesus to them? How would you proclaim Jesus's Kingdom of God to make it intelligible to them?

Jesus resorted to stories like the Prodigal son, the Good Samaritan, Lazarus and the rich man to get His message to the people. How do we know that those stories were true? To reveal Christianity to the "heathens' in Africa, the missionaries, when they first encountered those people did not proclaim that they are saved by the death of Jesus. They did not call them sinners. They did not tell them that Jesus was crucified on the cross to quell the anger of a God. To do so would encourage them to continue human and animal sacrifices to their Gods. The Catholic Churches offered Eucharist in Latin language at that time. Nobody knew what the Priest was saying. However, when translated in the native language, they were not told that the wine was the blood of Jesus and that the bread was His body. That would be counterproductive as the 'heathens' drank the blood sacrificed to their idols and ate the meat. Any interpretation of drinking the blood of Jesus and eating His flesh would encourage them to seek more human sacrifices as to drink their blood and eat their flesh after sacrifices. Looking back at the history of mankind, almost all practiced human sacrifices and cannibalism. The first African Christian was the Ethiopian eunuch, baptized by Philip. (Acts 8: 26-29) To get them to Christ, the Missionaries to Africa and other developing worlds also baptized the people. But the baptism was not for forgiveness of sins or for them to receive the Holy Ghost. The people never heard of Trinity or speaking in tongues after baptism. They baptized them with the loud proclamation-in the name of the Father, Jesus Christ and the Holy Ghost. The message to the Africans was loud and clear. Baptism makes one a Christian. Today, we know that water baptism does not make anybody a Christian. The Missionaries realized that the people were uneducated. The most impressive thing they did was to build schools, and of course churches. Then they preached the Gospel of Christ in the most elementary form that people could understand.

This was not the case for Paul. The Greco-Roman people were highly educated, among them philosophers like the Epicureans and the Stoics. To understand the methods that Paul used, you have to know something about him and his beliefs. This is not the place to give a complete biography of Paul or give a comprehensive documentary of his works in the Greco-Roman Empire. I have included in the bibliographies, the books that would guide the reader who is interested in the life and works of Paul. Paul, the greatest propagandist of Christianity, the man whose life after his Damascus experience, was patterned after Jesus's Kingdom of God. He was a student of Gamalial-a genius and distinguished Rabbi in the Jewish religion. Paul was well-versed in the Jewish concept of salvation, sin and redemption that featured prominently in the trajectory of the Jewish religion. The Jews resorted to sacrifices for the atonement of their sins as to obtain salvation. Like the other Jews, Paul believed in the original sin of Adam and Eve that all of us inherited. "By one man's disobedience many were made sinners." (Romans 5: 12, 18-19) He believed and was sure that if he had not sinned, that the risen Christ would not have saved him. Borrowing from his personal experience, Paul did something that was never heard since the world began: he proclaimed to the Greco-Roman people that they were all sinners and that the penalty of sin is death. "All have sinned and come short of the glory of God." (Romans 3:23) This dreadful nature of the Greco-Roman people was extended to all mankind. "We have before proved both Jews and gentiles that they are all under sin." (Romans 3: 9)

Paul's concept of sin and redemption looked at himself and all mankind and saw nothing but sin. That concept looked at the recorded history of the creation of Adam and Eve-as was known to him at that time-and reminded every one of the sins we inherited from them. Sin positioned itself at the birth places of all newborns and put a band on their wrists bearing the inscription-SINNER. You can see why all newborns cry and none ever smiled as they come out of the mother's womb into this world. Any newborn that refused to cry gets a slap on the butt as a reminder that the newborn is a sinner according to Paul. Even King David believed that he was born a sinner because his mother conceived him in sin. Many Evangelists today believe that we are all born in sin. Pauline doctrine of sin and redemption look at the face of God of Israel and saw nothing but anger and the demand for punishment. Jesus did not present to us a Father that is angry at mankind. He left no clue that His death was to quell the wrath and the anger of His Father.

On the day of the Pentecost, Peter accused the Jews that they killed Jesus. They asked Peter "what shall we do?" Peter said to them to repent and be baptized in the name of Jesus Christ for the remission of their sins. (Acts 2: 37-38) Jesus did not baptize any one for the remission of sins. Paul took a different approach when he told the prison guard "to believe on the Lord Jesus Christ and thou shall be saved and thy house." (Acts 16:31) He knew that the Romans had crucified Jesus, and yet, Paul did not accuse them of killing Him. Having convinced them that they were all sinners and the penalty of sin is death. In his letter to the Ephesians Paul told them they were dead in trespasses and sins. (Ephesians 2: 1) Paul did not give them the opportunity to ask "what shall we do?' He told them what to believe and what to do. His doctrine of sin and redemption took a quantum leap to Golgotha, revealing what Paul called the blessings and the glory of the death of Jesus Christ in many of his proclamations: "that Jesus came to the world to save sinners, of whom I am chief." (1 Timothy 1:15); that "Christ died for our sins according to the Scripture." (1 Corinthians 15: 3); "Jesus Christ, who gave Himself for our sins, that He might deliver us from the present evil world." (Galatians 1: 4)

It all seem a like a story, a myth if you may call it that. But what else could Paul have done as to bring a group of people, who never heard of Christ before to join him and be participants in the glory that Christ demonstrated. He got good results. Today many Evangelists are using the same methods. The Christian proclamation of 'faith' that Jesus came to the world to save sinners and brought salvation to them through His death epitomizes Paul's doctrine of sin and redemption. Today, things have changed. What worked for Paul two thousand years ago the tool we must use today. We have advanced our intelligence. We know, as I have revealed in this treatise, that that death and resurrection are grand stations on the trajectory path of human creation, that death is not evil. We know that the death of Christ did not wipe out the sins of the world. We know that not everyone in this world is a sinner, No newborn is a sinner. The Evangelists of today will tell you that if you deny that you are a sinner then you are unbeliever and not a Christian. That concept is a big obstacle to the new Christianity. It would seem that the gift of the Father offered to mankind was intended for sinners only. The death of Christ has nothing to do with sin. Jesus Christ gave no clue that He died for sinners. The big difference between Paul and today's Evangelists and many Christian leaders is this: while Paul was promoting his concept of sin and punishment, he lived like one who entered into Jesus's Kingdom of God. His earthly life style was an imitation of the life of Christ. He manifested his experience of that kingdom and saw his task from Christ as a labor of love for Christ, for His Father and for mankind. Like his Master, he left no house, no land, and no earthly treasures. Today's Evangelists and many Christian leaders, while proclaiming Paul's concept of sin and punishment live their earthly lives with no knowledge of that Kingdom. By their lifestyle examples of seeking power and accumulating earthly treasures, they have, like the Scribes and the Pharisees in the time of Christ, "shut up the kingdom of heaven against men: for ye neither go in yourselves, neither suffer ye them that are entering to go in." (Matthew 23:13)

Paul could not stop discussing his own sins. (Philippians 3:1-11) In carrying out his assignment from Christ, Paul did what he had to do. His doctrine of sin that he introduced to the Greco-Roman people represented the dark gloomy environment that had engulfed all mankind from which they cannot escape by themselves. Then he brought the light from Christ, through His death and resurrection and through faith in Him and His Father, to illuminate the world and save the wretched mankind. "But ye are not in the flesh, but in the Spirit, if so be that the Spirit of God dwell in you. Now if any man have not the Spirit of Christ, he is none of his. And if Christ be in you, the body is dead because of sin; but the Spirit is life because of righteousness. But if the Spirit of him that raised up Jesus from the dead dwell in you, he that raised up Christ from the dead shall also quicken your mortal bodies by his Spirit that dwelleth in you." (Romans 8: 9-11) This Spirit of Christ that 'dwells in you that shall resurrect your mortal bodies by His Spirit" is as I have pointed out in this treatise is Jesus's Kingdom of God in action.

Paul used the tools that were available to him. He read books on many subjects and could not do without his books. (2 Timothy 4:13) He knew the Jewish laws and customs better than the religious leaders. He borrowed from the Jewish beliefs mixed it up with his personal experience of Christ and used that knowledge to gain souls for Christ. It was tailored for the Gentiles. Today, would Paul use the same *modus operand?* The answer is no. To continue beating that drum today hides Jesus's Kingdom of God and the good news of His resurrection that Paul introduced to the Greco-Roman people. It is no longer necessary today to brand our newborns as sinners. Paul's aim was grandiose and lofty. He achieved the glorious victory for Christ and His Father and for humanity. Pauline doctrine of sin worked. However, once he reins the community in his chamber on that pretence, he reveals to them what salvation really means: the Spirit of Christ in human souls in action. It is what he experienced in himself with-"Christ in me." This is consistent with Jesus's Kingdom of God in action.

The ubiquitous way Paul piped this salvation to the Gentiles in the Greco-Roman Empire confused the early Christians who adopted his methods and transmitted them to us. When Pauline utterances are stripped of all his doctrines of sin, his personal experience as the chief sinner, what is left and what Paul proclaimed, is Jesus's Gospel, concentrating his efforts on Kingdom of God, His death and resurrection and the human destiny. Paul's earthly life, after his conversion, reveals itself as one who manifested his experience of Jesus's Kingdom of God. In the end, Paul puts all his utterances on atonement, redemption, and the sprinkling of the blood of Christ in a coffin and nailed it. Again, Paul did the impossible. He handed over to the Greco-Roman people what I labeled as Paul's cloned salvation to them: a salvation without the Torah, In this cloned salvation, Paul removed the God of Moses and replaced it with God, the Father of Jesus Christ; removed Moses as the Mediator and substituted Christ; redirected the future of this salvation to all the people of the visible and invisible Universe with some already in the third heaven. Although Paul bypassed Jerusalem as the new Kingdom of God on earth, he included his people as participant of the new glory of this salvation. The big question is this: how would you carry out that task as to achieve the same glorious end? The answer is not to use the doctrines of salvation, sin and punishment. But to disseminate the knowledge of Jesus's Kingdom of God and the vital truth on His epic miracle of the earthly stages of human creation. In doing so, the world community will gain knowledge of the Father, Jesus Christ, who we are, why we are here and where we are going. Perhaps, with this vital knowledge, mankind will see the thread that connects us as one common community and stop killing one another.

The story of Paul is the story of the journey of his soul with the Spirit of Christ to its glorious end. The platform that Paul used was the Greco-Roman Empire. His foundation was the Spirit of the risen Christ in his soul. The spectators were the Gentiles and some Jews. He drank his own cup. He was obedient to his call. Like his Master, he never fought back. There was no evil in his heart. During the grand demonstration, it was not Paul who lived but the Christ in him. Slowly, but aggressively, having inherited the free gift-that Spirit of Christ-that was not by his own will (1 Corinthians 6: 9-11; 15:20) Paul, experienced and manifested it as Jesus's Kingdom of God. With authority from Christ, Paul inaugurated Jesus's future Kingdom of God to everyone in Greco-Roman Empire and Asia Minor as salvation. Like the apostles, he found hope, righteousness, peace and joy in this Jesus's Kingdom. For Paul "the kingdom of God is not meat and drink, but righteousness, and peace and joy in the Holy Ghost." Paul died with the Kingdom of God within him. Paul looked forward for the promised eternal life with Christ and His Father.

For ye are dead, and your life is hid with Christ in God. When Christ, who is our life, shall appear, then shall ye also appear with him in glory.

—Colossians 3: 3-4

What Paul did not realize was that he executed all the requirements for the earthly phase of eternal life as was proclaimed, prescribed and demonstrated by Christ; that he took his last breath with that eternal life.

CHAPTER 12

JESUS'S ENCOUNTER WITH THE RICH YOUNG RULER (CONCLUDED)

The rich young ruler was invited by Christ to follow Him for the following reasons:

To listen to all Jesus's words on eternal life

To learn about the Kingdom of God and how to inherit it

To learn the pathways to earthly phase of eternal life that continues after death

To observe Jesus's everlasting miracle of the earthly stages of human creation

To learn how to participate in his own creation

To learn how to participate in sharing the nature of the Father

To learn how to experience and manifest that experience to the world.

To see the prototype of the fully created spiritual being that was showcased on Easter

To observe the final scene of Jesus's epic miracle of human creation on the day of

Pentecost.

To learn how to obey the will of the Father and the commandments of Christ

To have knowledge of the Father and Jesus Christ

To have knowledge of the Gods creating human beings

Learn how to develop and build a solid foundation on how to believe in them.

The rich man declined and went away sorrowfully. He was not prepared to sell all his good and give everything to the poor. The inheritance of Jesus's Kingdom of God opens the portal of many divine elements in the Spirit of His Father available to those who entered into that Kingdom. One of them is the divine elements of the nature of the Father that made us partakers in the nature of His Father for those who entered into that vast paradise of the Kingdom in human souls. When the divine elements of the nature of Father is activated, deployed and put into action, we will be as perfect as the Father. It manifests externally with love that extended to the enemy, compassion, forgiveness, mercy and the zeal to obey the Father's will and the commandments of Christ. Jesus went to cities and villages preaching and demonstrating the earthly phase of eternal life and the nature of His Father by His earthly life style. The epitome of the earthly life of Christ is the mirror through which we see the deeper reflections of the nature of God, our Father. Jesus gave practical demonstrations of the nature of His Father and the eternal component of eternal life in His Kingdom of God by His epic miracle of the earthly phase of human creation. Jesus used it to reveal the meaning of eternal life and His role in human creation. By using Himself as the model, the Game is over for all research for the Gods creating human beings and who controls the intrinsic human life.

Eternal life is a priceless possession. It is that Pearl of Great Price that a merchant man, seeking goodly pearls found and he went and sold all that he had and bought it. (Matthew 13:45) It is again like the Hidden Treasure that a man found and for joy, sold all he had and bought it. (Matthew 12:44) The young rich man missed the greatest show on earth and denied himself access to the vital information on who the Father is, who Jesus is, what human life is and the destiny of mankind. He was one of the unwilling guests invited to the Wedding Feast. (Matthew 22:1-10; Luke 14:16-24) The words of Christ to the rich man, were like seeds that fell among the thorns in the parable of the Sower. "The cares of the world, the deceitfulness of riches and the lusts of other things entering in choked the words and it became unfruitful. (Mark 4:18-19)

The story of the young rich ruler at a glance looks like the story of rejection of Christ and His Kingdom of God. On deeper reflection, what it revealed is that earthly treasure is the great obstacle to what Christ prescribed and proclaimed, that is still prevalent today worldwide. It is an enlarging pothole along the trajectory of the earthly phase of human creation that must be repaired as we accept the gift of eternal life from the Father through Christ, as we embark on the journey to the glory that awaits all mankind. The quest to accumulate earthly treasures leaves no room for inheritance of eternal life or for our participation in the earthly phase of our creation.

What shall it profit a man (who must die) *if he gains the whole world* (the earthly treasures of the world) *and loses his soul?*

—Jesus. Mark 8:36

And seek not ye what ye shall eat or what ye shall drink, neither be ye of doubtful mind. For these things do the nations of the world seek after; and your Father knoweth that ye have need of these things. But rather seek ye the kingdom of God and all these things shall be added unto you. Fear not, little flock; for it is your Father's good

pleasure to give you the Kingdom. Sell all you have, and give alms;
provide yourself bags which wax not old, a treasure in heaven that
faileth not, where no thief approacheth, neither moth corrupteth..
For where your treasure is there will your heart be also. Let your
loins be girded about and your light burning.

—Luke 12:29-35

Follow Me.

—Jesus

Jesus's metaphoric expression, "Follow Me" is an invitation to seek to enter into His Kingdom of God for the revelations of the end-less mysteries of the Father and Himself. It makes it easier to know who Jesus Christ is and the Father that He revealed to the world. It revealed the most important purpose of the Father for mankind and the relationship of Jesus with the Father. The Light that shines in the darkness and we could not comprehend, became compre-hensible. It revealed along the radiant divine beam in its trajec-tory, the mysteries and the power of Jesus's kingdom of God, His divinity and His creative powers, the intrinsic value of human life, the glorious destiny of the human soul, our role in the earthly phase of human creation and the ultimate infinite relationship of human souls with the Spirit of the glorified risen Jesus Christ and His Father.

Jesus had already called His apostles to follow Him. They all obeyed and witnessed all the epic demonstrations. That invitation is still open to us to participate and win the trophy of eternal life through Jesus's Kingdom of God. Let us start with the zeal to gain knowledge of the Father and Jesus Christ as to comprehend the epic demonstrations that reveal the meaning of eternal life and the role of Christ in human creation, if you are willing to follow

Him. In His last days, Jesus rode into Jerusalem, riding on a colt. We must follow Him every day. It is a journey of no return to life without Christ. "No man, having put his hand to the plough, and looking back, is fit for the Kingdom of God." (Luke 9:62) It is a journey that will take you through multiple earthly stages of creation to the spiritual worlds of Jesus and His Father. There are spiritual stations along the trajectory of this life journey. Death is one such grand station the human souls must pass through as to harness the glory of the fully created spiritual mankind. How to enter into Jesus's Kingdom of God and inherit eternal life, and what to do after you have inherited it, was prescribed by Him in His teaching and demonstrated by His earthly lifestyle. Why we need to enter into that eternal life was demonstrated by His everlasting miracle of the earthly stages of human creation. Jesus used Himself as the model. In doing so, Jesus revealed the creative power of the Spirit of His Father in Him and His role in human creation.

I am the Resurrection and the Life.

— Jesus. John 6:25

BIBLIOGRAPHY

Adams, Marilyn M. *Horrendous Evils and the Goodness of God*. Ithaca: Cornell UP, 1999.

Armstrong Karen. *A History of God*. Ballantine Book. NY. USA 1993

Anderson, Hugh, ed. *Jesus*. Englewood Cliffs: Prentice-Hall, Inc., 1967.

Aulen, Gustaf. *Dag Hammarskjold's White Book*. Philadelphia: Fortress Press, 1969.

Barclay, William. *Jesus as They Saw Him*. Grand Rapids: William B. Eerdmans Company, 1962.

Beasley Murray. *Jesus and the Kingdom of God*. The Paternoster Press. UK 1986

Bornkamm, Günther. *Jesus of Nazareth*. Trans. Irene McLuskey and Fraser McLuskey. Minneapolis: Fortress P, 1995.

. *Jesus the Human life of God*. Forward Movt. Publication. Ohio. USA. 1987

Borsch Fredrick. *God's Parable*. The Westminister Press Philadelphia. USA 1975

Bright John. *The Kingdom of God*. Abingdon Press. USA 1953

Brown, Raymond E. *The Death of the Messiah*. Vol. 2. New York: Doubleday, 1994.

Burton, Trochmorton Jr. *Gospel Parallels*. Nashville: Thomas Nelson Publishers, 1979.

Candlish James. *The Kingdom of God Biblically and Historically considered*. HardPress Publishers. Miami, Fl. USA. 1882

Carus, Paul. *The Gospel of Buddha*. Chicago: Carus Company, 2004.

Cooper, Terry D. *Dimensions of Evil*. Minneapolis: Fortress P, 2007.

Davies, Oliver, trans. *Eckhart: Selected Writings*. London: Penguin Books, 1994.1961

Davis Stephen et al *The Resurrection* Oxford University Press. USA 1997

Dodd C. H. *The Parables of the Kingdom*. Charles Scribner;s & Sons. USA

Donahue John. *The Gospel in Parables*. Fortress Press. USA 1990

Dych William. *Thy Kingdom come*. Herder and Herder Books. USA 1999

Emerson, Harry Fosdick. *The Man from Nazareth*. New York: Harper and Brothers, 1949.

Enumah, Festus. MD. *The Innocent Blood and Judas Iscariot*. Guardian Books: Canada, 2002.

Enumah Festus MD. *The Father's Business and the Spiritual Cross*. Published in Charleston. USA 2014

Fallows, Samuel Rt. Rev. *Bible Encyclopedia and Scriptural Dictionary*. Chicago: The Howard-Severance Company, 1907.

Ferguson Sinclair. *The Holy Spirit*. InterVasity Press. ILL. USA. 1996

Fite Warner. *Jesus the Man*. Harvard University Press. USA. 1946

Forde, Gerhard. *On Being a Theologian of the Cross*. Grand Rapids: William B. Eerdmans Comp., 1997.

Fosdick Harry. *The Man from Nazareth*. Harper and Brothers. NY. USA 1949

Fuellenbach John. *The Kingdom of God*. Orbis Books. NY. 1995

Goguel, Maurice. *Jesus and the Origin of Christianity*. Vols. 1 & 2. New York: Harper Torchbooks, 1960.

Gordon, D. Kaufman. *In Face of Mystery*. Cambridge: Harvard University Press, 1995.

Gordon Kaufman *Jesus and Creativity*. Fortress Press. USA 2006

Gunton C. E. *Christ and Creation*. William Eerdmans Publishing, USA 1992

Häring, Bernard. *The Law of Christ*. Trans. Edwin G. Kaiser. Westminster: The Newman P, 1963.

Harnack, Adolf. *What is Christianity?* New York: Harper & Brothers Publishers, 1957.

Harnack Adolf. *Marcion and the Gospel of Alien God*. Wipf and Stock Publishers. USA 2007

Hengel, Martin. *Crucifixion*. Philadelphia: Fortress P, 1977.

Hick, John. *Death and Eternal Life*. Louisville: Westminster/John Knox P, 1994.

Hick John *Evil and the God of Love*. Palgrave Macmillian Press USA 1977

Hoenig, Sidney B. *The Great Sanhedrin*. Philadelphia: Bloch Publishing Co. 1953.

Holland Henry Scott. *God's City and the coming of the Kingdom*. Longmans, Green & Co

NY. USA 1987

The Holy Bible, Original King James Version. Gordonsville: Dugan Publishers Inc., 1985.

Jackson Samuel Macauley. *The new Schaff-Herzog Encyclopedia of Religious Knowledge*.

Baker Book House. Grand Rapid. Michigan. USA 1950

Jeremias Joachin *Jerusalem in Times of Jesus*. Philadelphia: Fortress Press, 1969.

Jeremias, Joachim..*The Parables of Jesus*. Prentice-Hall. USA 1963

Kaufman Gordon *God the Problem*. Harvard University Press. USA. 1972

Kaufmann Walter (Introducer) *Religion from Tolstoy to Camus*. Harper Torch Books. N.Y. 1961

Kim Kirsteen. *The Holy Spirit in the world*. Orbis Books. NY. USA 2007

Kittay, Eva F. *Metaphor*. Oxford: Clarendon P, 1989

Ladd George. *The Gospel of the Kingdom*. William B. Eerdmans Publishers. USA

Lakoff, George, and Mark Johnson. *Metaphors We Live By*. Chicago: University of Chicago P, 1980.

Linwood Urban *A short history of Christian thoughts*. Oxford University Press 1995.

Lockyer, Herbert. *All the Messiah Prophecies of the Bible*. Grand Rapids: Zondervan Publishing House, 1960.

McConkie Jeseph et al. *The Holy Spirit*. Bookcraft. Utah. USA 1989

McInerny, D. Q. *Being Logical*. New York: Random House, 2004.

Meeks, Wayne A., ed. *The Writings of St. Paul*. New York: W. W. Norton & Company, Inc., 1972.

Moltmann Jurgen. *God in Creation*. Fortress Press. Minneapolis. USA 1993

Nelson-Pallmeyer. *Jesus against Christianity*. Harrisburg, Penn.: Trinity Press International, 2001.

Norman Beck. *Mature Christianity in the 21st Century*. Crossroad. NY, USA 1994

O'Malley Williams. *God the oldest Question*. Loyola Press. ILL. USA 2000

Pelikan, Jaroslav. *Jesus Through the Centuries*. New York: Harper & Row, 1985.

Pink Arthur. *The Beatitudes and the Lord's Prayer*. Baker Books. USA 1979

Richards, Lawrence O. *The Word Bible Handbook*. Waco: Word, Inc., 1982.

Sanday, William. *The International Critical Commentary on the Holy Scripture of the Old and New Testaments*. New York: Charles Scribners Sons, 1920.

Schillebeeckx, Edward. *Jesus: An experiment in Christology*. New York: Seabury, 1979.

Sheen, Fulton J. *Life of Christ*. New York: Image Books Doubleday. 1958.

Schweitzer Albert *The mystery of the Kingdom of God.* Dodd, Mead Publishers. USA 1914

Simkhovitch, Vladimir. *Toward the Understanding of Jesus.* New York: The MacMillan Company,1925.

Spong John Shelby. *Liberating the Gospels.* HarperSan Francisco. USA 1996

Stott, John. *The Cross of Christ.* Downers Grove: InterVarsity P, 1986.

Thompson Marianne Meye. *The Promise of the Father.* Westminister John Knox Press. USA. 2000

Tolstoy Leo. *The Kingdom of God is within you.* University of Nebraska Press USA. 1984

Townshend, George. *The Heart of the Gospel.* London: Templar Printing Works, 1939.

Toynbee, Arnold. *The Crucible of Christianity.* New York: The World Publishing Company, 1969.

Wesley John. *The nature of the Kingdom.* Bethany House Publishers. USA. 1979.

Wilson, Ian. *Jesus: The Evidence.* New York: Harper Collins Publishers, 1984.

Wood, et al. *Immanuel Kant: Religion within the Boundaries of Mere Reason And Other Writings.* Cambridge: Cambridge UP, 1998.

Dr. Festus Enumah has arranged for part of his share of the proceeds from all his books to be donated to Samuel A. Enumah Africancer Foundation, www.africancer.org, a public, charitable nonprofit 501(c) (3) corporation registered in the state of Georgia, USA. The objective of the foundation is to help develop and build the infrastructure in sub-Saharan Africa for cancer control services, focusing on cancer education, prevention, early detection and treatment. The aim of the foundation is to help reduce the deaths from cancer and improve cancer patients' quality of life.

ABOUT THE AUTHOR

Dr. Festus Enumah is a surgeon who trained at Cook County Hospital in Chicago and at the University of Texas M. D. Anderson Cancer Center. He attended college in Nigeria at the University of Ibadan Medical School and Government College.

Dr. Enumah is the founder and president of the Samuel A. Enumah Africancer Foundation. This American nonprofit plans to build sustainable cancer detection and treatment centers in sub-Saharan Africa and is working on a model to serve all patients—regardless of level of income. In addition, Dr. Enumah and his wife, Lois Bronersky-Enumah (also a physician), have spent time in Nigeria running a free medical clinic.

Enumah enjoys golf and tennis as well as collecting Bibles and rare books on Christianity. He and his wife have four children.

Dr. Enumah's other books include *The Innocent Blood and Judas Iscariot* and *The Father's Business and the Spiritual Cross.*